# WOMEN AND FAMILIES

# WOMEN AND FAMILIES

EDITED BY JACOB NEUSNER

WIPF & STOCK · Eugene, Oregon

Wipf and Stock Publishers
199 W 8th Ave, Suite 3
Eugene, OR 97401

Women and Families
Edited by Neusner, Jacob
Copyright©1999 by Neusner, Jacob
ISBN 13: 978-1-59752-504-6
ISBN 10: 1-59752-504-9
Publication date 10/12/2007
Previously published by The Pilgrim Press, 1999

CONTENTS

Preface  *vii*
Contributors  *xi*
Publisher's Note  *xii*
Introduction · JACOB NEUSNER  *xiii*

1  Islam · JONATHAN BROCKOPP  *1*
2  Christianity · BRUCE CHILTON  *26*
3  Judaism · JACOB NEUSNER  *50*
4  Hinduism · BRIAN K. SMITH  *82*
5  Buddhism · CHARLES HALLISEY  *106*

Literary Sources of the World Religions  *139*
Notes  *157*

PREFACE

The great world religions address certain existential issues in common, for the human situation raises compelling questions that transcend the limits of time, space, and circumstance. Recognizing that each religion forms a system with its own definitive traits, we aver that all religions must and do treat in common a range of fundamental topics as well, and we hold that comparison and contrast among religions begins in the treatment of urgent questions that all of them must resolve. This library introduces the religions of the world as they meet in conversation on the profound issues of world order—transcendent, individual and familial, and social. In the first rubric falls how we know God; in the second, our life of suffering and death, women, and the aspiration for afterlife;, and in the third, the authority and continuity of tradition itself. Indeed, for the purpose of these volumes we may define religion as a theory of the social order that addresses from the unique perspective of transcendence (God, in concrete language) issues of the human condition of home and family on the one side, and issues of the public interest on the other.

The five topics of the initial account require only brief clarification. Common to the human condition is the quest for God. Every religion identifies authoritative teaching ("sacred texts"), though what the various religions mean by "a text" will vary, since a person or a drama or a dance as much as a piece of writing may form a fixed and official statement for amplification and exegesis through time. One half of humanity is composed of women. Everyone suffers and everyone dies. Humanity everywhere aspires to explain what happens after we die. In these five volumes, the initial set in the Pilgrim Library of World Religions, we take up the five topics we deem both critical and ubiquitous in the religions we identify as paramount. Following a single outline, worked out in common, we spell out how each religion addresses the topic at hand. In this way we propose to make possible a labor of comparison of religions: how all address a single issue, uniformly defined.

The religions are chosen because all of them not only speak to humanity in common but also relate in concrete, historical ways. Judaism, Christianity, and Islam join together in a common doctrine, the unity of God, and in valuing a common scripture, the Hebrew Scriptures of ancient Israel that Judaism knows as the written Torah—which is the Old Testament of Christianity, joined in the case of Christianity and Islam into the Bible, the book, comprising the Old and New Testaments. Hinduism forms the matrix out of which Buddhism took shape, much as ancient Israelite Scriptures amplified by the Judaism of the day defined the matrix in which Christianity originated. Not only do Judaism, Christianity, and Islam conduct an ongoing dialogue between and among themselves, but Christianity and Islam compete in Africa, and Hinduism and Islam in India. All five religions not only address humanity but reach across the boundaries of ethnic groups and local societies and speak of the condition of humanity. And all five come to formulation in a set of writings deemed classical and authoritative.

That fact—that each of the religions treated here identifies a canon that defines the faith—makes the work possible. For each of the religions treated here proves diverse; viewed over time, all of them yield marks of historical change and diversity of doctrine and practice alike. Take Judaism, for example. Today it breaks down to a number of distinct religious systems or Judaisms—Reform, Orthodox, and Conservative in North America, for instance. Christianity yields three vast divisions,

Catholic, Protestant, and Orthodox. The world has gotten to know some of the differences between Shiite and Sunni Islam. The upshot is that while we recognize the density and diversity of each of the religions under study in these volumes, our account of their principal doctrines on critical and universal issues appeals only to those writings that all forms or versions of the several religions acknowledge, to which all Judaisms or Christianities, for instance, will appeal.

That same fact—the appeal to authoritative writings of a classical character—also permits us to describe without nuance of context or historical circumstance the positions of the five religions. People who practice the religions set forth here may believe diverse things within the framework of those religions, respectively; Catholics may practice birth control, for example. So too, religions that bear a distinctive relationship to a given ethnic group—Judaism to Jews, for instance—cannot be defined merely by public-opinion polling of that ethnic group. Not all Jews practice Judaism, not all Arabs Islam, nor all Italians Catholicism. By concentrating on the classical statements of the religions at hand, we set forth an ideal type, the picture of the religion that its authoritative writings provide, not the picture of the religion that the workaday world may yield.

The same consideration affects the diversity over time and in contemporary life of the several religions before us. Everyone understands that all five religions not only produced diverse systems, but also developed and changed over time, so that a doctrine or belief on a given topic in one time and place may not conform to the shape of the same doctrine or belief on the same topic in a different setting. For example, ideas about God vary, depending on the situation of the interpreter—learned or mystic or simple, for instance—or on the age in which the idea is explained. That is quite natural, given the vast stretches of time and space traversed by the five religions we examine. While acknowledging the variations produced by the passage of time and the movement of culture, we appeal to the classical writings for an account that all later generations of the faithful, wherever located, can affirm, however diverse the interpretations placed upon that account. In the section "Literary Sources of the World Religions," found at the back of the book, each of the writers lists the documents that form the foundation of his chapter in this volume.

This library took shape in the shared intellectual adventure that joins us together as professors of the academic study of religion at Bard College and in dialogue with our students there, and we tried out the various chapters on those students. The chapters were outlined in common.

All of us express our appreciation to the president of Bard College, Dr. Leon Botstein, and dean of faculty Stuart Levine for their encouragement of this project; and to Richard Brown, then of Pilgrim Press, our patient and gentle editor, whose good ideas always made the work still more challenging and stimulating than our joint venture had made it to begin with.

Jacob Neusner
SERIES EDITOR

CONTRIBUTORS

JONATHAN BROCKOPP received his Ph.D. from Yale University. He is assistant professor of religion at Bard College.

BRUCE CHILTON is Bernard Iddings Bell Professor of Religion, departmental chair of religion, and chaplain at Bard College. He is rector of the Free Church of St. John the Evangelist.

CHARLES HALLISEY is John L. Loeb Associate Professor of the Humanities at Harvard University.

JACOB NEUSNER is distinguished research professor of religious studies at the University of South Florida and professor of religion at Bard College.

BRIAN K. SMITH is professor of religious studies at the University of California, Riverside.

## PUBLISHER'S NOTE

The Pilgrim Press is a leading publisher in Christian ethics and theology. Through the Pilgrim Library of World Religions series, edited by Jacob Neusner, we seek to continue and expand this heritage.

Part of this heritage is a policy regarding the use of inclusive language for human beings and for God. With few exceptions, the Pilgrim Library of World Religions maintains this heritage. Nevertheless, we recognize that various religious traditions have struggled differently with inclusive language for God. Therefore each contributor, especially when discussing God's self-revelation, has been offered some flexibility in order to faithfully reflect that religious tradition's current form of expression.

# INTRODUCTION

A religious system says the same thing about many things. Each religious system is comprised by a way of life, worldview, and a theory of the social entity that embodies that way of life and explains itself by appeal to that worldview. In this way the religious system constructs for the faithful a coherent social order. Therein the faithful find self-evidently valid answers to a coherent set of questions. And, since the questions take shape in all the diverse dimensions of life and the answers repeat the same basic proposition, the critical components of a system serve equally well to portray the character of the system, viewed whole. If, therefore, we want to characterize Judaism or Islam or Christianity or Buddhism or Hinduism, we should find it possible to work from the detail to the whole.

How each of these religious traditions deals with women and families will then form a laboratory case of how they respectively deal with other critical topics. A case in point is how the great world religions speak about that half of their communicants comprised by women. If we know how to ask the system's questions in general, we will be able to understand what each of the religious systems has to say about women and family in particular. The self-evident importance of the theme needs no exposition. Throughout the world religious communities, challenged by women to reorder matters involving women's roles and interests, rethink long-established attitudes and policies. That is why the theme of the present part of this series enjoys self-evident relevance to contemporary culture. At the same time, since we wish to inform ourselves about the classical and normative views of the five world religions treated here, the topic affords the opportunity to ask scholarship to illuminate a critical contemporary issue. And from the viewpoint of the task at hand—to undertake the comparative study of world religions—no more appropriate occasion for systematic comparison can present itself. For one given of every religious system is uniform: women, children, and family comprise much of the present and define all of the future of every religion that aspires to continuity.

Since every religious system deals with women and families, we are able to compare and contrast the several systems, for in the present aspect, all of them are talking about the same thing. That creates a possibility of comparison of like to like that we do not always have. If, for example, the religious traditions do not share in common a given category, such as revelation, or if they define a given category in very different terms, such as afterlife, comparison proves uncertain. We do not always know that we are comparing like to like to define difference. But if, as in the present case, we know with reasonable certainty that the religious traditions concur on fundamental points of definition, and if we know issues each addresses are congruent with those important to the others—relationships of husbands and wives, parents and children, generations past and future—then illuminating comparison and contrast become feasible.

What that means is, when we ask the same questions to all five world religions at hand, we deal with what ought to be a topic of critical concern to each one of them. That, then, defines a level plane, a common framework, for comparison and contrast. The reason is, in all five instances we are talking about the same thing. Then, when differences present themselves, we may be sure that the differences mark what is, in each case, the same systemic component. On the surface, when we speak of God or of evil and suffering or of Scripture, we may be using words that mean one thing in one setting, something else or nothing at all in another setting, so a nontheistic religion such as Buddhism and an incarnational theism such as Christianity meet and match only with some difficulty. But when it comes to women, the biological and economic and social phenomena, e.g., childbearing, remain comparable.

And that simple observation brings us to the promise of this volume in comparing religions. In theory we should be able to identify important traits of a religious system if we generalize from the way it portrays norms for women, defining the virtuous woman, acceptable deviations from the ideal, unacceptable deviations, and the public role of women in work, politics, and the religious life. If we treat the information organized in these categories as indicative of the concerns of the system as a whole, then we should find in the case at hand that the system signals its deepest concerns. The data should underscore the urgent questions a system asks and the self-evidently valid answers it proposes for those questions. The challenge of this book therefore takes two parts. First, we want to treat the theme of women as systemically exemplary. So we ask ourselves, how does the presentation of women in the systemic writings deliver the larger systemic message? Second, we wish to deepen our grasp on the theme by comparing and contrasting the treatment of the subject by the several systems. So we wonder what is to be learned when we see how the same topic is presented by the several systems considered in these pages.

That is the key to what we hope to contribute. By seeing choices made by the several systems, we gain perspective on the selections made by one religion and not by another. Only when we see Islamic or Buddhist or Judaic or Hindu or Christian models of feminine virtue—not only on their own, but also side by side—do the distinctive traits of Islam, Buddhism, Judaism, Hinduism, and Christianity emerge in sharp relief. That involves ways in which the several religions differ, but also ways in which they are the same. All concur that a particular set of virtues characterize the good woman, vices the bad, and these virtues and vices concern women in particular, not only "humanity" (meaning men) in general. Then the definition of the virtues to be nurtured, with their matching vices to be avoided, will attest to larger concerns that preoccupy the system as a whole. At that point the work of comparison takes over: which virtues, and why these and not some others? Here one system contributes perspective on the others, showing us choices that can guide a particular system's treatment of the subject shared among all five.

But virtue does not stand alone. A positive charge that a woman ought to exhibit these traits over the life cycle attracts a negative one, which concerns deviations from the (ideal) norm. The virtuous woman may be the good daughter, the faithful wife, the nurturing mother. Then what should we say of the woman who remains celibate? And what about the childless woman? Spinsterhood too challenges the norm. So matters prove more nuanced than they appear on the surface. Then how do the several religions define and sort out matters of gender variance? Finally, we move beyond the circle of home and family and encompassing household to women in public life. Women not only bear and raise children (so the five religions under discussion here concur), they also do useful work, both in and out of the household. They hold and act on political opinions. They undertake public roles within the religious life and in ritual affairs. So we turn to women in public spheres of the social order contemplated by the religions studied here.

Whether in Orthodox Judaic or Islamic circles or in Roman Catholic Christianity, in Eastern and in Western countries, the status and role of women come under debate. Feminists within Islamic circles appeal to the model of the Prophet's circle, where, as Professor Brockopp points out, "women of the early Muslim community were celebrated paragons of the new faith." So, too, while the virtuous woman remains in seclusion,

Islam makes provision for public roles as well. Christianity began with a position in opposition to the conventional family and in favor of ample recognition of women, as Professor Chilton shows. The special interest of Professor Chilton's presentation lies in his interest in the exemplary uses of women in systemic analysis: "During the survey, we will pay special attention to how a given model was generated by its underlying vision of human life." So nothing is to be treated in isolation, but everything attests to the larger context that sustains and nurtures a given view. When we come to Judaism, we find that the woman's virtues define the ideals of public conduct for Israel in an unredeemed world: humility and forbearance, which the system itself labels as feminine, are what Israel must exhibit. Then, in the world to come, man's virtues succeed. The hero had the strength to overcome his impulses; self-denial and accommodation, in attitude and emotion—these represented the norms for all Israel, the holy community of which Judaism speaks. For his part, Professor Smith underscores the conflicted views of women—pillars of society but weak and untrustworthy, objects of reverence but driven by lust, dependent but aggressive. Given the exceptional complexity of Hindu society, we may hardly find surprising the diverse and conflicting views of women that come to expression in the life of the Hindu pantheon as well: "Hinduism provides a set of different kinds of religious, moral, and social ideals for women, each with its own set of possibilities and ambivalences." Finally, in Professor Hallisey's account, two conflicting ideals govern: "those that acknowledge sexual difference and those that ignore gender in favor of a fundamental egalitarianism with respect to spiritual ability." But he concludes with a cogent resolution of the conflict: "models of virtue for women *as women* are also important models of virtue for men *as human beings*." And that conclusion draws us back, in a circuitous route, to the message that

Judaism wishes to set forth, a message that Islam and Christianity and important elements of Hinduism certainly will affirm—but each in its own way and in its own idiom.

This brief review of what is to come underscores the challenge of reading this book. Here the authors follow a common program, each with his distinctive data trying to address a single set of questions. The common program facilitates contrast and comparison. We are able to construct a single continuum, placing the five religions in five places along a single line. At the same time, if we wish a deeper understanding of any one of the five religions, we will want to ask ourselves two more questions. First, how do the indicative traits of each system come to expression in the topic at hand—Judaism's interest in the formation of a holy community to accomplish God's purposes in creating humanity, something Adam failed to achieve, or Christianity's goal of forming Christ's church in imitation of the founder? What have the teachings concerning women to do with these larger systemic commitments? Second, what do we learn about the five systems from the respective choices that each makes in response to the challenges at hand: defining virtue, sorting out difference, and dealing with public life of the social order, all with reference to women.

CHAPTER 1

# *Islam*

The construction of women in Islamic society has become the subject of intense debate. Whom one picks as representing the model is hotly disputed, and how one reads the historical record is often more revealing of one's political agenda than it is of the evidence. But whether feminist or traditionalist, reformer or conservative, the background of every Islamic discussion of women is the Qur'an and the stories of the Prophet and his companions. The Qur'an addresses the status of women directly in numerous passages, not surprisingly, since the women of the early Muslim community were celebrated paragons of the new faith. Their example makes clear that the central requirements for Muslim women (just as for men) are belief and obedience.

Before turning to the stories of these important women, it is necessary to understand the framework set out by the Qur'an. When Muslims differentiate between equality of men and women in terms of faith, and equality in social roles, they continue in the same tradition as the Qur'an; women are seen as equal on one level, but different on another. As for equality in terms of faith, the Qur'an specifically states women are responsible for their own salvation; they cannot depend on the faith of their husbands to save them on Judgment Day (see 3:192–93). So men and women are the same in terms of faith, but they differ in terms of their physical attributes and their place in

Muslim society. In the following verses, differences between men and women are emphasized through the example of menstruation, and this biological model leads to women being compared to fertile fields plowed by the man.

> They will question thee concerning the monthly course. Say: "It is hurt: so go apart from women during the monthly course, and do not approach them till they are clean. When they have cleansed themselves, then come unto them as God has commanded you." Truly, God loves those who repent, and He loves those who cleanse themselves.
>
> Your women are a tillage for you; so come unto your tillage as you wish.
>
> —The Cow, 2:222–23[1]

This passage seems to emphasize a woman's passive role, both in terms of her body and in terms of her husband's desire for sex. Another verse is even more direct in addressing the differing status of women and men:

> Men are the managers of the affairs of women for that God has preferred in bounty one of them over another, and for that they have expended of their property.
>
> Righteous women are therefore obedient, guarding the secret for God's guarding.
>
> —Women, 4:38

Rules of marriage and inheritance are also directed toward men, who are seen in the role of providing for women and protecting them. But the Qur'an also grants specific rights to women, including ownership of property and rights of inheritance.

Such rights, important as they are, still do not tell a Muslim woman how she is to live. To address this question, the Qur'an mentions a number of women throughout history who serve as examples for the faithful. These include Mary, the mother of Jesus; Sarah, the wife of Abraham; and the wives of the Prophet. The fact that all these women are mentioned due to their association with a male prophet speaks to the derivative nature of their influence. But while women are never prophets in the Qur'an, neither are their roles insignificant.

## MODELS OF VIRTUE FOR WOMEN THROUGH THE LIFE CYCLE

Because the Qur'an is regarded as the last of the three great revelations (after the Torah and the Gospels), Jewish and Christian figures appear in the Qur'an as Muslim prophets. The Qur'an does not tell the story of individual prophets in a single narrative; rather, tales of prophets from the Hebrew and Christian scriptures are interspersed with tales of Arabian prophets and other material. Moreover, individual tales are repeated several times in the Qur'an. The resulting effect is that the story of Sarah and Abraham, for instance, does not appear as something out of ancient history but rather as a reminder of God's constant, active presence in these believers' lives. The following passage notes four models for women, two for unbelievers and two for believers.

> God has struck a similitude for the unbelievers—the wife of Noah, and the wife of Lot; for they were under two of Our righteous servants, but [their wives] betrayed them, so they availed them nothing whatsoever against God; so it was said, "Enter, you two, the Fire with those who enter."
>
> God has struck a similitude for the believers—the wife of Pharaoh, when she said, "My Lord, build for me a house in Paradise, in Thy presence, and deliver me from Pharaoh and his work, and do Thou deliver me from the people of the evildoers."

And Mary, Imran's daughter, who guarded her virginity, so We breathed into her of Our Spirit, and she confirmed the Words of her Lord and His Books, and became one of the obedient.
—The Forbidding, 66:10–12

In all of these examples, women play active roles in relation to their husbands. The unbelieving women are not supportive of their husbands' faith, while the believing women cling to their faith in the face of adversity. Moreover, Mary, along with the righteous women in the previous verse, is singled out for her obedience to God. These brief remarks are typical for the Qur'an, and short, vague references may have sufficed an audience already familiar with longer versions. For instance, the story of Abraham and Sarah is quite detailed in the Hebrew Scriptures (Genesis 18:1–15). Here, Abraham receives guests who tell him that his wife will bear him a son, and Sarah overhears this tale from behind the tent wall and laughs, since she is far too old to bear children. In the Qur'an, however, she confronts the guests:

And [Abraham's] wife was standing by; she laughed, therefore We gave her the glad tidings of Isaac, and, after Isaac, of Jacob.
She said, "Woe is me! Shall I bear, being an old woman, and this my husband is an old man? This assuredly is a strange thing."
They said, "What, dost thou marvel at God's command? The mercy of God and His blessings be upon you, O people of the House! Surely He is All-laudable, All-glorious."
—Hood, 11:74–76

The fact that Sarah addresses the guests directly instead of hiding demurely in the tent as in Genesis may reflect the relative license granted to older women in many Islamic cultures. Here, age is an asset, and older women often gain a measure of independence from the strictures of cultural expectations. More important, Sarah is instructed to trust God, who is more knowledgeable of these affairs than she. So while Sarah receives her message directly from the visitors, her role is not one of prophet but of faithful believer who is to trust in her Lord's message.

Of the other women in the Qur'an (the queen of Sheba, wife of Potiphar, and a few others), the role of Mary, mother of Jesus, is most fully developed as an ideal for emulation. Her faith in the face of persecution is exemplary, and she also receives prophecy and direct contact with angels. Although Jesus is the prophet, he is much less prominent than his mother, and the Qur'an refers to the events of his life only obliquely. Mary, in contrast, receives an entire sura, which begins with the announcement of John the Baptist's birth to Zachariah. Arberry, our translator, likens this sura to a medieval Christmas carol and maintains this feeling by dividing up the verses in a rhythmic fashion.

> And mention in the Book Mary
> when she withdrew from her people
> > to an eastern place,
> and she took a veil apart from them;
> then We sent unto her Our Spirit
> that presented himself to her
> > a man without fault.
> She said, "I take refuge in
> the All-merciful from thee!
> > If thou fearest God . . ."
> He said, "I am but a messenger
> come from thy Lord, to give thee
> > a boy most pure."
> She said, "How shall I have a son
> whom no mortal has touched, neither
> > have I been unchaste?"
> He said, "Even so thy Lord has said:
> 'Easy is that for Me; and that We

may appoint him a sign unto men
and a mercy from Us; it is
   a thing decreed.'"

—Mary, 19:16–21

While Sarah's rejection of God's prophecy centered on her advanced age, Mary defends her honor, as someone who could not conceive since she had never slept with a man. Like Sarah, she is told to trust in God, and so after she conceives she withdraws from her family and bears the child alone to avoid the shame. Mary's trust in God is rewarded, for when she comes back to her home with the new child in tow, they accuse her of being unchaste, but she shows them a sign that marks Jesus as a true prophet:

Then she brought the child to her folk
carrying him; and they said,
"Mary, thou has surely committed
   a monstrous thing!
Sister of Aaron, thy father was not
a wicked man, nor was thy mother
   a woman unchaste."
Mary pointed to the child then;
but they said, "How shall we speak
to one who is still in the cradle,
   a little child?"
He said, "Lo, I am God's servant.
God has given me the Book, and
   made me a Prophet.
Blessed He has made me, wherever
I may be; and He has enjoined me
to pray, and to give alms, so
   long as I live,
and likewise to cherish my mother;

> He has not made me arrogant,
> unprosperous."
>
> —Mary, 19:28–33

Jesus' first act as a prophet, therefore, is to defend Mary's honor and assert that she should be venerated. Amidst a background of family life, where Sarah and Mary are bound up in the tasks of caring for husbands and children, they are given revelation and judged by their faith in God. The importance of childbearing as a central part of a Muslim woman's identity is emphasized in these stories. While it is clear that their status in the community is derived from that of men, no man could perform the unique duties of faith assigned to them. These stories also provide an important context for other Qur'anic injunctions, which might otherwise be interpreted as legislating an utterly passive role for women.

Historically, this emphasis on the importance of family is interesting in light of the fact that the Prophet himself was an orphan. Not surprisingly, then, Islamic law urges the care of all members of the community, particularly those who are not protected by family structures. Such customs make a place for widows and orphans, but do not necessarily care for those who break with social norms. Mary, for instance, should not be taken as an example for having children out of wedlock, since the Qur'anic punishment for illicit sexual intercourse is one hundred lashes. Further, a woman who does not bear children may face divorce or the possibility that her husband will marry another wife. In such cases, she might be sent back to her family in disgrace. This power of divorce is placed almost entirely in a man's hands, and even the Prophet threatened his wives with divorce on occasion.

The Prophet's wives are addressed directly in the Qur'an, separated out from the rest of the believers and made into examples for others. Known as the "mothers of the believers,"

Muhammad's wives played important roles in the early community. It was his first wife, Khadija, who helped Muhammad determine that he was being visited by an angelic spirit and not a devil when he first received the revelation. Muhammad did not marry another wife as long as Khadija lived, but after her death in 619, he took on several more wives to solidify certain friendships and treaties. By all accounts, 'A'isha, the daughter of his close friend Abu Bakr, was his favorite. Muhammad married her when she was just a girl, and she outlived him by many years. Much is known about 'A'isha, and some have argued that with the many stories recorded about her life with the Prophet, we have the makings of the first Muslim autobiography.

When the Qur'an addresses the wives of the Prophet, though, it admonishes them for not taking their roles seriously enough. Like Sarah, they should restrain themselves and be obedient to God:

> Wives of the Prophet, you are not as other women. If you are godfearing, be not abject in your speech, so that he in whose heart is sickness may be lustful; but speak honourable words.
>
> Remain in your houses; and display not your finery, as did the pagans of old. And perform the prayer, and pay the alms, and obey God and His messenger.
>
> —The Confederates, 33:32–33

Part of what it means to be an ideal is to be set apart from others, so a new set of morals is enjoined on the wives of the Prophet in order to distinguish them from the actions of women before the coming of Islam. While there is no evidence to suggest that most Muslim women were held to this ideal of seclusion in their homes, the very existence of this as a model for virtue has meant that women's actions are constantly seen as falling short of these pious goals.

It is possible that the Prophet's wives were not entirely

happy with these arrangements, since elsewhere the Qur'an threatens them with divorce if they do not hold to the ideals set for them. One should not overemphasize the social requirements placed on these women, however, since lists of pious behavior expected from Muhammad's wives emphasize religious behavior, particularly the ideals of surrendering one's will to God and acting out one's belief through devotion and fasting.

Beyond the wives of the Prophet, there were other women who were held up as being especially virtuous. Sumayyah bint Kubbat, a slave who was tortured to death by her master when she refused to deny her faith in the new Islamic religion, was the first of many martyrs who gave their lives for Islam. And Muhammad's daughter Fatima is the ideal woman for Shi'ites particularly, since they venerate the family of the Prophet. As the mother of the grandsons of the Prophet, and wife of the Prophet's cousin Ali, Fatima retained an important position in the early community. Shi'ites see her as preferable to 'A'isha because although Fatima was involved in political decisions, she did not take on political leadership. Rather, Fatima is revered for her spiritual authority and her commitment to her family.

Islamic history holds many other examples of women who put their faith in God above all other duties and ideals. Rabi'a al-'Adawiyya (d. 801) has been particularly important to Muslim women who seek to follow the mystical path of Sufism. Rabi'a devoted herself completely to worship of God and left aside all other forms of attachment. Known as a second Mary due to her vow of celibacy, she wrote poetry that emphasized her devotion to God. The following lines have been attributed to Rabi'a, and she supposedly recited them when refusing an offer of marriage.

My peace, O my brothers, is in solitude,
And my beloved is with me always,

For His love I can find no substitute,
And his love is the text for me among mortal beings,
When-e'er His Beauty I may contemplate,
He is my "mihrab," towards Him is my "qibla"
If I die of love, before completing satisfaction,
Alas, for my anxiety in the world, alas for my distress,
O Healer (of souls) the heart feeds upon its desire,
The striving after union with Thee has healed my soul,
O my Joy and my Life abidingly,
Thou wast the source of my life and from Thee also came my ecstasy.
I have separated myself from all created beings,
My hope is for union with Thee, for that is the goal of my desire.[2]

Rabi'a's utter devotion to God meant that she rejected both family and the role of seclusion, preferring to wander the streets of Basrah, preaching openly. While Rabi'a's example is unusual, it is not unique. Thousands of female mystics are recorded in the sources, and Sufism allows a certain freedom of action for women. Even today women still run and maintain female mystical orders in Syria and elsewhere. In medieval Cairo these orders provided a place of refuge for women who needed to escape a difficult family or social situation, or who had nowhere to go in their old age.

As is clear from these examples, there is not one ideal for Muslim women to follow, but many varying possibilities. While all of them place devotion to God as the centerpiece of a Muslim woman's life, devotion to the husband and family can be secondary. The reason for the wide variation in Qur'anic models of virtue is probably due to variations in Islamic society at the time. In Arabia, female goddesses were often the most important heavenly powers and were served by female oracles and priestesses. We know that some women were wealthy, such as the Prophet's first wife, Khadija, and some were known as great poets. Certainly, men occupied most public roles, but of seventy-five who represented the delegation of new Muslims from Medina in 622, two were women, and of those who fought in the early skirmishes with the unbelievers, a number of women warriors are recorded. Further, some Medinan tribes were matrilinear, taking their family and clan heritage through their mother's line instead of their father. What is shared in these models is belief and obedience; the simplicity of these injunctions—and of the Islamic model for virtue in general—makes them appropriate for all Muslim women.

## DEVIATIONS FROM THE IDEAL

In 1438 a devastating plague hit Cairo. The sultan met with the religious scholars, and they determined that the plague was a punishment from God due to a loss of morality in society. In response, the sultan ordered that women be barred from going out in the streets. The sultan's order reflected a sense that Muslim women were deviating from the norms set for them in the Qur'an, and their enforced seclusion was an attempt to turn them back to pious devotion and obedience. Many Muslim conservatives today see Western cultural imperialism as similar to the Cairo plague; so like the sultan, they see women's behavior as the first thing to rein in.

But how one determines deviations from the ideal actions of the Prophet's wives and daughter depends very much on how one interprets the Qur'an and Islamic law. In the fourteenth century a jurist named Ibn al-Hajj (d. 1337) wrote a book in which he berated the women of Cairo for straying from the ideal; but rather than use the example of Sarah, Mary, or the Prophet's wives, he viewed women as naturally deficient in reason and rich in animal sensuality. In an article on Ibn al-Hajj, Huda Lutfi writes:

Muslim prescriptive literature viewed the female body primarily as the repository of male sexual pleasure, and hence a source of temptation that should be concealed; Ibn al-Hajj's treatise is no exception. . . . Properly concealed, women might cease to be a threat to the social order. Yet female clothes were also viewed as serving the function of adornment for the husband's sexual pleasure.[3]

This dichotomy between publicly enforced asexual behavior and private sexual behavior is built on a philosophical model for women as associated with the irrational world of emotion and sex, resulting from their animal soul having precedence over their rational soul. Ibn al-Hajj writes:

> [Women] are deficient in mind and religion, and therefore, they are permitted to use silk, gold, silver and other such items because of their deficiency. As for the man, he is the repository of perfection, God has perfected and adorned him, so he is not allowed to indulge in the adornment permitted to those who are deficient.[4]

While Ibn al-Hajj can cite the Qur'an to support his argument, his model of virtue is one that is quite different from that found in the Qur'anic stories of Mary and Sarah. Moreover, it seems to have been an ideal few women in his time were living up to.

Ibn al-Hajj's book has remained quite popular, and many of the ideals he expressed are still taken up by more conservative elements among Muslims. In the modern period, the South Asian conservative scholar Abu al-A'la Maududi is one of those who has repeated this criticism of women for deviating from the ideal. Viewing calls for liberation from the veil as Muslim weakness in the face of colonialist pressures, he turns a critical eye toward Western civilization, seeing genocide, child abuse, and homosexuality as rooted in the freedoms given to women. His response is to have the laws of *purdah,* or separation between the sexes, enforced, calling on the example of the Prophet's daughter:

> These commandments [of purdah] are meant not only for the other people but also for the servants of the house. Once Hazrat Bilāl or Hazrat Anas asked Hazrat Fātimah, daughter of the Holy Prophet, to hand him her child. She handed it by stretching her hand from behind a curtain, where both these gentlemen were the personal attendants of the Holy Prophet, and lived with him like the other people of his house.[5]

Maududi's point is that Fatima was so careful about preserving her piety that she did not even allow her servants to see her. Using the Prophet's wives as examples, however, also leads Maududi to support education for women.

> Women have not only been allowed to obtain education in religious and mundane branches of knowledge, but their education and cultural training has been considered as important as that of men. Women also used to take lessons in religion and morality from the Holy Prophet along with men, though they had separate arrangements for the purpose. The wives of the Holy Prophet, especially Hazrat 'Ā'ishah, not only taught women, they taught men also. Many an illustrious Companion and follower of the Companions learnt the *Qur'an, Hadith,* and Islamic Jurisprudence from Hazrat 'Ā'ishah.[6]

It can be argued that Maududi is only interested in Islamic models of virtue so far as they serve his purposes of secluding women. However this may be, it is important to note that there is no Qur'anic basis for the idea of equality between men and women in any sense beyond the equality of belief before God. Men and women are seen as essentially different in the Qur'an, with different roles in public and in the household. Specifically, men are the managers of the affairs of women, have the right to divorce, and generally inherit at a higher rate than women. While modern legal codes have obviated some of these rules, particularly restricting polygamy and the right to have concubines, this ideal of differentiated roles is still visible in many Muslim societies.

In calling the wives of the Prophet the "mothers of the believers," the Qur'an both solidifies their roles as exemplars and defines the way in which they are to be exemplars: not as bearers of revelation or political leaders, but as mothers. But while Muhammad's wives were held up as exemplars, their actions were not always exemplary. In fact, the wives of the Prophet played numerous roles in early Muslim society. Tradition holds that one wife, Hafsa, kept one of the few written versions of the Qur'an, and this version was the basis of the authoritative text we have today. Another wife, 'A'isha, was enormously influential in the establishment of the early community, openly taking political positions and leading an army into battle in 656. In fact, Muhammad's first wife, Khadija, was the only of these "mothers of the believers" who actually bore Muhammad a child (Fatima) who would live to bear him grandchildren.

Curiously, it was Muhammad's favorite wife, 'A'isha, who most often deviated from the ideal. One of the best-known stories attached to 'A'isha is the affair of the lie. It seems that when she was about fifteen she fell behind a caravan returning to Medina and got lost. When she eventually got back to town, it was in the company of a handsome young man. Tongues began to wag, and many people questioned her honor. An early source relates the story in 'A'isha's own voice.

> I [left the caravan] for a certain purpose, having a string of Zafār beads on my neck. When I had finished, it slipped from my neck without my knowledge, and when I returned to the camel I went feeling my neck for it but could not find it. Meanwhile the main

body had already moved off. I went back to the place where I had been and looked for the necklace until I found it. . . . I returned to the place [where the caravan had been] and there was not a soul there. The men had gone. So I wrapped myself in my smock and then lay down where I was, knowing that if I were missed they would come back for me.[7]

At this point 'A'isha is found by a young man, who seats her on his camel and walks deferentially behind her. Knowing that she had done nothing wrong, 'A'isha does not give the matter further thought.

Then we came to Medina and immediately I became very ill and so heard nothing of the matter. The story had reached the apostle and my parents, yet they told me nothing of it though I missed the apostle's accustomed kindness to me. When I was ill he used to show compassion and kindness to me, but in this illness he did not and I missed his attentions.[8]

Finally, the Prophet came to visit 'A'isha and asked her to confess to the crime that others accused her of committing. She refused, knowing that she had done no wrong.

He sat down and after praising God he said, "'Ā'isha, you know what people say about you. Fear God and if you have done wrong as men say then repent towards God, for He accepts repentance from His servants." As he said this my tears ceased and I could not feel them. I waited for my parents to answer the apostle but they said nothing. . . . When they remained silent my weeping broke out afresh and then I said: "Never will I repent towards God of what you mention. By Allah, I know that if I were to confess what men say of me, God knowing that I am innocent of it, I should admit what did not happen; and if I denied what they said you would not believe me. . . . I will say what the father of Joseph said:

'My duty is to show becoming patience and God's aid is to be asked against what you describe.'"[9]

Muhammad struggled with these accusations while 'A'isha suffered, awaiting her fate. Finally, God sent a revelation to Muhammad (24:11–13) that cleared 'A'isha's name.

It is clear that not everything 'A'isha did is to be considered an ideal for other Muslims to follow. But after the Prophet's death, she was one of the most important of the early companions, and her involvement in the Battle of the Camel (in 656) is one of the most controversial events in early Muslim history, partially because of her status as mother of the believers. After the murder of the third caliph (leader of the Muslims after Muhammad's death), the Muslims were divided as to who should be their leader. Some named 'Ali, the husband of Muhammad's daughter Fatima, while others supported the companions Talha or Zubayr. Eventually, 'A'isha led this group of dissenters into battle against 'Ali, directing the fighting from on top of her camel, hence the name of this the first battle that pitched Muslim against Muslim.

As a result of that battle, many Muslims died and 'A'isha herself was captured and put under house arrest. One modern author, al-Afghani, sees this event as a warning to all who would accept women as political leaders.

> The Battle of the Camel is a beacon in the history of the Muslims. . . . It is ever present in their minds to put them on guard any time there appears among them a tendency to blindly imitate other nations by claiming political rights for women. . . . The memory of 'A'isha should be pondered more than ever in our day. It never ceases saying to the Muslim: Look how this endeavor failed in the very heart of our Muslim history! We don't have to repeat it senselessly.[10]

In contrast, Fatima Mernissi, a Moroccan sociologist, argues that not only should 'A'isha's behavior be tolerated but also that it establishes a precedent for women's role in politics. Questioning al-Afghani's account of 'A'isha's behavior as aberrant, she writes: "The Prophet's wives did not seem to regard political or military problems as being alien to them. They were as much concerned with the liberation of prisoners, an eminently political matter, as with domestic questions."[11] This battle, some thirteen hundred years ago, serves as the basis for an ongoing argument about women's place in public life. For now, it is only necessary to note that one person's model of virtue for a Muslim woman is another's deviation from the ideal.

Throughout Islamic history women have pushed the boundaries of acceptable action, and exceptions were always made for women of wealth or power. For instance, Zubayda, the favorite wife of Caliph Harun al-Rashid, built aqueducts in Mecca to bring more water to the pilgrims. Further, Shajarat al-Durr (reigned 1250–58), a one-time slave in the court of Cairo, took control of political power and was the first woman to have coinage struck with her name listed as ruler. Shajarat al-Durr's reign was opposed by the imperial court in Baghdad, and they supposedly sent a messenger to say, "If you cannot find a man to rule you, let us know and we will send you one." Yet for eight years this deviation from the norm was accepted, and Shajarat al-Durr's legacy is still visible in the huge stone mausoleum complexes she built for her husband and herself.

Although leader of Egypt in her time, Shajarat al-Durr was never cited as an example for other Muslim women. While her rule was tolerated, and perhaps ignited the dreams of some, the religious community did not hold her up as an ideal to be copied. In the modern period, however, it is possible to locate women who simultaneously function as role models yet violate the very norms they espouse. Two of these women are the world-renowned singer Umm Kulthum and the founder of the Muslim Women's Association, Zaynab al-Ghazali.

Umm Kulthum (1904–1975) became one of the most popular singers in the Arab world. Raised in a small village in rural Egypt, her first vocal training was in the chanting of the Qur'an, as taught to her by her father. As a girl, she was in great demand and accompanied her father in tours through the various villages of her region. But while such roles for a girl were unusual, they were more tolerable than if she had been an adult. When Umm Kulthum decided to continue her singing career after reaching a marriageable age, her troubles began. In an interview, she recounts the years when she performed in boys' clothes.

> Though life seemed good to me, I could tell that my father was uneasy. The idea that his daughter should be a singer was a difficult thing for him to accept. His son, yes, but a daughter, ah, that was something else, and besides I was growing up. So he began to dress me in boys' clothes, a *zibun,* or long vest, over the *jallabiyah* (or full-length garment) and on my head the *iqal* and the *kuffiyah.* I sang in this garb for several years. I realize now that my father wanted to deceive himself, to postpone in his mind what he was doing, letting his daughter sing in public. And he also wanted to deceive the audience and convince them that the singer was not a young girl but a young boy.[12]

Once beyond this difficulty, Umm Kulthum gained legendary popularity in the Arab world due to her singing traditional religious songs and putting ancient Arabic poetry to tune. Though she married, she never had children, devoting her life solely to her singing career. Umm Kulthum clearly deviates from Ibn al-Hajj's norms, as well as those of Maududi, yet her personal piety and the beauty of her voice allowed her to transcend the normal limitations required of pious women.

Another example from current history is Zaynab al-Ghazali (b. 1917), one of the few women to gain a leadership role among the Muslim Brotherhood, a group whose goal is to reestablish Islamic law as the basis of society. Trained in Qur'an, Hadith, and preaching, she used to give weekly lectures to some three thousand women in a Cairene mosque; she also spent a number of years in jail on suspicion that she was involved in a plot to assassinate the leader of Egypt. Zaynab al-Ghazali's life is a study in contradiction, for though she urged women to follow the traditional roles of caring for children and family, she divorced her first husband because he interfered with her life of religious activism. She wrote:

> Women [are] ... a fundamental part of the Islamic call. ... They are the ones who build the kind of men that we need to fill the ranks of the Islamic call. So women must be well educated, cultured, knowing of the precepts of the Koran and Sunna, informed about world politics, why we are backward, why we don't have technology. The Muslim woman must study all these things, and then raise her son in the conviction that he must possess the scientific tools of the age, and at the same time he must understand Islam, politics, geography, and current events. He must rebuild the Islamic nation. ... Islam does not forbid women to actively participate in public life. It does not prevent her from being anything, as long as that does not interfere with her first duty as a mother, the one who first trains her children in the Islamic call.[13]

In a later interview, al-Ghazali revealed that she saw her childlessness as a blessing from God, which allowed her, unlike other women, to devote time to political work.

As has been noted, such deviations were accepted for a variety of reasons, but class and wealth certainly made these allowances more palatable. In addition to these exceptions, it is interesting to note who in Islamic society is never held to these ideals. The text of Ibn al-Hajj seems to confirm modern sociological observances that different standards have been held for the lower classes, where requirements such as the veil and seclusion are not stringently applied. In fact, he praised lower-class women for selling wares from door to door so that other women could stay at home. Similarly, slaves, although Muslim, were held to a different standard, often functioning as necessary intermediaries between secluded women and the outside world. In general, one can assume wide variations in Islamic cultures that cover a tremendous geographical scope, from North Africa to Southeast Asia. This tolerance of local culture is itself an expression of the Islamic ideal, which developed a legal system dependent not on a central authority but on the learning of individual scholars of the law. Within this system, local custom, or *'urf,* had an important place in forming the face of Islamic law in that area. So while the Qur'an enjoins all believers, men and women, to be modest in their dress, what constitutes modest dress in one part of the world may differ from another.

Finally, while deviations from the ideal are to be found everywhere, equally ubiquitous are the examples of women who live on the edge of Muslim societies, forgoing the requirements of modesty or piety for economic or social reasons. Such women have included sorceresses and prostitutes, and at various moments in history they have played powerful roles in society. By living beyond the pale of acceptable activity, they both define the limits of a pious Muslim woman's behavior and enable the middle- and upper-class woman to fulfill the pious ideal.

## WOMEN AND PUBLIC LIFE

If, in the minds of conservatives like Maududi, the Muslim ideal for women is one of a pious, devoted mother who secludes herself from the gaze of strange men, the antithesis of that ideal is the prostitute, who walks the streets openly and does not protect her family's honor. In other words, the ideal of secluded chastity sets up a dichotomy between virgin and whore that makes life difficult for those women who would seek public office in Muslim countries. As in contemporary Western society, women are held to different standards than men. Yet one should not assume that the public worlds of Christian and Muslim society are the same.

Public life in the Islamic world is separated into several specific spheres. For instance, political leadership of the community is generally centralized in one figure, while religious leadership is fundamentally decentralized, spread among leaders of the many different religious and teaching institutions found in the major cities. Among the religious institutions are mosques of various sizes and importance, each with a prayer leader who might also serve as the muezzin (who calls the believers to prayer) and as an instructor in Qur'anic recitation. Islamic mystical orders often have their own structures, where novices might live with their families as they pursue the spiritual path with their guide. Separate institutions might also be erected for the court of the Islamic judge *(qadi)*, who oversees questions ranging from land disputes to divorce to inheritance, or for the *mufti*, who gives nonbinding opinions on questions of Islamic law.

Educational institutions are likewise varied in size and scope. On the elementary level, *kuttabs* are erected for studying Arabic and Qur'an recitation. More advanced education is pursued either in special mosques, known as *madrasas*, in which Islamic law, theology, and tradition are taught, or in a variety of other institutions. These latter range from private libraries to the homes of famous philosophers or medical doctors who would teach the non-Islamic sciences.

Commercial activity is also regulated by Islamic law, and most of this occurs in the public market (bazaar or *suq*). These central areas of stores are often organized according to the specific wares, with leather merchants in one section and booksellers in another. Buying and selling also are carried out by traveling merchants, who hawk their wares from door to door, and by those who undertake long-distance or international trade.

There are, of course, many other spheres of public life, but this short list is sufficient to note the number of different areas that must be addressed when looking at the question of women in the public sphere. According to Ibn al-Hajj's model, women would be involved in none of these spheres, yet even he breaks this rigid pattern along lines of class, noting the importance of (lower-class) female vendors, who travel from door to door to allow (upper-class) women to purchase the necessary items for their homes without ever leaving them.

Ibn al-Hajj's mention of these vendors suggests that while men generally had more public involvement than women, certain roles were also accorded women. Some of these traditional, semipublic roles include farming and selling vegetables. Further, although it is rare to see women as shopkeepers, they have always contributed to the economic well-being of their families, whether through production of handicrafts in the home or traditional professions reserved for middle-class women: midwifery, matchmaking, undertaking, etc. Again, seclusion from the world of men does not necessarily include seclusion from the society of women, and in many Muslim countries it is a woman's responsibility to find suitable spouses for her children. Further, it is often the women of the two households who meet to discuss the proposal of marriage.

While access to these public spheres is difficult, historically women have been involved in all of them, even those of political leader and mufti. This fact is far more representative of the elasticity of Islamic norms, however, than it is of any sense of equality. While the Qur'an states that the labor of one is as the other (3:193), men occupy almost all of these public roles. Where women have been accepted is in roles exclusively involved with other women, and even extremely conservative governments support the training of female doctors to treat women, or female scholars to teach women. While conservative women veil themselves in front of strange men, women are at complete freedom in each other's company and never veil or cover themselves in front of other women. For instance, while living in a conservative Iraqi village in the 1950s with her husband, Robert, Elizabeth Femea observed a *kraya,* a Shiite prayer service led by a woman for the sake of women:

> Ramadan had been under way for a week when Mohammed asked me if I would like to go to an evening kraya with his sister Sherifa. It would be a big kraya, he said, held in the house of a distant relative.... Bob had already been to several krayas for men, and I was eager to go, for the women talked about the krayas as great social as well as religious events.... The kraya, Sherifa said, would begin about half past eight. It was still only seven-thirty, but fifteen or twenty women and numerous children were already present. I had never seen any of the women of ahl-es-suq before, the shopkeepers' and artisans' wives, and I watched them as they filed in, greeted old friends, and kissed with deference the older women present.... There was a stir: the mullah had arrived, a tall woman with a hard, strong face, carrying worn copies of the Koran and her own Book of Krayas. Everyone made way for her as she strode across the court and seated herself ceremoniously in the chair near us.[14]

While krayas are only found among Shi'ite Muslims, they are typical of the separate educational and religious structures that may be open to women in conservative cultures. For instance, Zaynab al-Ghazali taught thousands of women in Cairo, and Maududi invoked 'A'isha's example for education of women in

Pakistan. In other parts of the Muslim world, women may even serve as spiritual guides for men.

For example, the leader of the new Islamic Republic of Iran, Imam Khomeini (d. 1989), gave an extensive series of lectures on Islamic government in 1970. In these lectures, he cites Fatima as the preferred example for Shi'ite Muslims but distinguishes her spiritual authority from her right to rule. Khomeini, who was born on Fatima's birthday, was one of the most conservative Islamic leaders in recent history, yet he still cites Fatima as an authoritative source for guidance on the nature of government.

> The Prophet himself said: "We have states with God that are beyond the reach of the cherubim and the prophets." . . . Fatima also possessed these states, even though she was not a ruler, a judge, or a governor. These states are quite distinct from the function of government. So when we say that Fatima was neither a judge nor a ruler, this does not mean that she was like you and me, or that she has no spiritual superiority over us.[15]

In this way, Khomeini demonstrates the same dichotomy expected of women in Sunnite communities. Although Fatima is seen as superior in her spiritual power, and may therefore have an influence on government, she does not rule directly.

## CONCLUSION

This chapter has focused on conservative thinkers and movements in Islam, from Ibn al-Hajj to Maududi and Khomeini, not because their views are the most authoritative but rather to emphasize that even the conservative extreme sees important roles for women in some aspects of public life. In contrast, Muslim feminists have argued that the Prophet wished to establish a radical equality between men and women in all public spheres. Like Ibn al-Hajj, their project of reinterpretation of the early sources leads to a deviation from the Qur'anic ideal, but by using the recorded actions of women like 'A'isha to define how a Muslim woman should act today, they demonstrate the continuing power of these models of virtue. This new movement to increase the role of women's public and religious roles includes efforts in South Africa to open up judgeships of the Islamic courts to women and attempts to find a basis in Islam for universal human rights. Such movements are certain to open a new chapter in the role of women in Islam.

Finally, the reassertion of Islamic identity by Muslim feminists may be seen as a reassertion of the most important tenets of the ideal Muslim woman: faith in God and obedience to the religion. Although Sarah laughed at the announcement of her upcoming child and Mary faced charges of unchastity, each maintained their faith in God and was obedient to his commands. This same faith is the one tie binding the various examples of Rabi'a, Zaynab al-Ghazali, and Fatima Mernissi as all continue to struggle with the ancient sources in forging a new identity for Muslim women.

CHAPTER 2

# *Christianity*

During the nearly two millennia of its development, Christianity has insisted upon very different standards in the comportment of the sexes and in the ordering of families. Such differences are natural in a religious perspective that has been involved in the drastic social changes Christianity has seen. But the fact that Christian views of sexuality and family have changed in no way diminishes Christianity's categorical insistence upon sexuality and family as vital aspects of how the people of God are to live within the Spirit of God. In this topic more than in others, Christianity presents a paradox: changes of standards on the one hand, and categorical insistence upon current standards on the other hand. And both the changes and the insistence exert an immediate impact on the understanding (and the self-understanding) of women.

To understand this paradox, we will consider four representative—and at one time or another dominant—models of sexuality and family. Our survey will by no means be comprehensive, but it should give us a sense of the range of models involved. Arranged by their emergence in time, the four models are:

1. Opposition to the conventional family, and re-evaluation of women (in Jesus' teaching and primitive Christianity)
2. The embrace of family, the silence of women (in early Christianity)

3. The transformation of sexuality into gender, of family into society (in orthodox Christianity)
4. The contention over gender (in contemporary Christianity)

During the survey, we will pay special attention to how a given model was generated by its underlying vision of human life unfolding in the presence of God's spirit. That will permit us, in the conclusion, to see how the paradox of constant change in this realm, together with categorical insistence upon the centrality of sexuality and family, in fact represent a coherent feature of Christianity.

Because Jesus and the Gospels prove to be foundational for subsequent developments in Christianity (in this and other matters), we will turn to the first model by way of introduction. The second model will then show us how Christianity evolved models of virtue for women; the third amply illustrates the necessity for revolutionary departures from that ideal; and the fourth brings the contemporary dispute about women in public life front and center.

## INTRODUCTION

There are rather clear indications that Jesus and his family were on strained terms. Within Mark (3:31–35), for example, we encounter the following scene:

> And his mother and his brothers come and standing outside, they sent a delegation to him, calling him. And a crowd sat around him, and they say to him,
>
> Look, your mother and your brothers and your sisters seek you outside.
>
> He replied and says,
>
> Who is my mother and my brothers?
>
> He looks around at those sitting in a circle about him, and says,

Look: my mother and my brothers. Whoever does the will of God, he is my brother and sister and mother.[1]

Not a picture of family bliss, and perhaps an echo of the earlier statement (3:21) that there were those associated with Jesus who tried to prevent him from engaging in exorcism. They said he was "beside himself." Now he says they are not true family.

The assertion involved in Mark 3:31–35 insists upon an explicit principle: the bonds of family are to come second to the will of God. It is much more than an anecdote concerning a particular dispute. There are such anecdotes in the New Testament, for example in John 7:1–13. In that case, Jesus and his brothers fight over whether he should go to Jerusalem for the feast of tabernacles. He adamantly refuses their invitation, but then in fact goes to Jerusalem secretly. The circumstantial quality of the narrative is interesting, but the bold assertion in Mark 3:35 is all the more trenchant by contrast.

It is common in the study of the New Testament always to read such statements of principle as simple assertions of the value of certain social structures, such as the church, above that of the family. And it is true that, within the development of faith the New Testament represents, that understanding did emerge. We find it clearly expressed (in Jesus' name), for example, in the Gospel According to Matthew (10:34–41):

> Do not presume that I came to put peace on the earth! I did not come to put peace—but a sword! Because I came to separate man against his father, and daughter against her mother, and bride against her mother-in-law, and the man's enemies will be his house-members! The one who loves father or mother more than me is not worthy of me, and the one who loves son or daughter more than me is not worthy of me, and whoever does not take his cross and follow behind me, is not worthy of me. The one who has found his life will forfeit it, and the one who has forfeited his

life for my sake will find it. The one who receives you receives me, and the one who receives me receives the one who delegated me. The one who receives a prophet in the name of a prophet will receive a prophet's reward, and the one who receives a righteous man in a righteous man's name will receive a righteous man's reward.

This is a well-crafted speech that represents the perspective of the church after the resurrection: the picture is for people to follow Jesus in the way of the cross, and to put the fellowship of those sent in his name—the name of a prophet and just man—ahead of any call upon familial loyalty.

But prior to what happened to Jesus in Jerusalem, the church had no real organization, no comprehensive structure as a conscious replacement of ordinary relationships. So it will not do to imagine Jesus as replacing the family with another structure of society. The problem with such readings is that the Galilee, which was the context of Jesus' movement for most of his life, was grounded fundamentally in the family as the ordinary unit of social life. A village such as Nazareth consisted only of between four and five hundred people, and it made its way as an agricultural service community. The pivotal role of the family is summarized by Richard A. Horsley:

> Villages consisted of a smaller or larger number of families or households. As the most fundamental social form in a traditional agrarian society, the household was the basic unit of production and consumption. According to the Israelite ideal (similar to that of other peasantries), each family worked and lived from the produces of its ancestral inheritance of land. Each household produced most of what it consumed and consumed much of what it produced. As indicated by both rabbinic texts and archaeological excavations, within the village settlement each family lived in a "house" of a small room or two ($3 \times 4$ m) opening off of a court-

yard shared with one or more other families. In the courtyard they shared use of oven, millstone, and cistern. In the village they shared use of a common wine-press and olive press.[2]

Within the setting that the study of the social context of Galilee has permitted us to appreciate clearly for the first time, Jesus' radical rejection of the bonds of family becomes all the more startling.

He was not in the position, for example, of claiming that urban institutions—such as the Temple or a Pharisaic association or the Roman army—superseded the family. Such urban institutions were not a feature of his programmatic activity, and he did not have significant contact with any city, with the exception of Jerusalem (and then, his contact brought about his execution). In *Evil and Suffering*, the previous volume of the Pilgrim Library of World Religions series, we have already seen how Jesus understood the kingdom of God as a divine power in the process of transforming the world as it can be seen and known.[3] Part of the transformation included the dissolution of the ordinary bonds of family, which were widely experienced as a fundamental category of social life.

Jesus' radical challenge of the place of loyalty to family explains another, famous aspect of his message. He insisted upon including women among his followers and authorizing their participation in the process of learning (so Luke 10:38–42):

> As they traveled he entered a certain village; a certain woman named Martha received him. And her sister, called Miriam, sat at the Lord's feet and heard his word. But Martha was distracted with much serving, approached and said, Lord, does it not matter to you that my sister has left me alone to serve? Speak to her, then, so that she comes to my aid! But the Lord answered and said to her, Martha, Martha, you care and worry and fret about many

things, but one is necessary. Because Miriam has chosen the good part, which will not be removed from her.

Passages of this kind were cited during the debate in England concerning the ordination of women, and a case to some extent on biblical grounds did prevail.[4] But here, too, one must not presume that Jesus is offering a structure of society (or of church). Rather, the word of the kingdom is such that it dissolves the usual constraints, including the constraints of family and sexuality, in the brilliance of its vision of God. If God is in the process of transforming the world and us with it—which is Jesus' understanding of the kingdom—then nothing must stand in the way of the transformation.[5]

More than twenty years after Jesus' execution, Paul—in his letter to the Galatians (written around 53 C.E.)—insisted upon a cognate principle (Gal. 3:28): "There is neither Jew nor Greek, neither slave nor free, neither male nor female, because you are all one in Jesus Christ." That widening of Jesus' principle, to include the removal of ethnic and economic boundaries, as well as of sexual boundaries, has provided Christianity with a strong sense of the autonomy of human conscience, collective and individual, in the ordering of society. That helps to explain the revolutionary developments in the understanding of sexuality and family which have been characteristic of Christian thought.

## MODELS OF VIRTUE FOR WOMEN THROUGH THE LIFE CYCLE

The second Christian century was a time of profound ferment within the church. The definition of Christianity as distinct from Judaism was widely agreed on the part of Jews and Christians and representatives of the Roman Empire, and that made for a sense of beleaguered cohesion. Christians could no longer claim the right as Jews not to take part in the, for them idolatrous, worship of the image of Caesar, and that made for a persistent environment of persecution.[6] On the other hand, the definition as being apart from Judaism pressed Christians into the arena of philosophical debate with many other ways of looking at God (Judaism included), a debate which was then very popular.[7] They gave accounts to outsiders and to one another of how their way was the way the one God would have humanity live.

No work was more popular among Christians at this time than *The Shepherd of Hermas*. Jaroslav Pelikan is representative of scholarship in his description of the apocalypticism of *The Shepherd of Hermas:*

> The author (or authors) of the Shepherd used the format of an apocalyptic summons to call the readers to repentance. The vividness of its eschatological language is exceeded only by the decisiveness of its plea. The Lord had not yet returned, and therefore the work of judgment was not yet complete; but it would soon be finished, and then the consummation would come.[8]

As Pelikan points out, his use of the word *apocalyptic* here does not refer to the hard-and-fast distinction between this world and the world to come. Rather, a process started within the world is pointed toward its eschatological completion. In fact, the line of demarcation between the present and the future is less sharply drawn in *Hermas* than it is, say, in the Revelation of John in the New Testament (which was written around 100 C.E.).

In the first vision of *Hermas* (chap. 1), an angelic lady appears to Hermas and accuses him of sin (specifically, of impure thoughts about a woman, whom the angelic lady resembles). Her analysis of the rewards that attend righteousness, and therefore of the punishments that await evil, is succinct (*Shepherd* I.1.8):

> For the righteous man has righteous designs. As long as his designs are righteous, his repute stands fast in heaven, and he finds the Lord ready to assist him in all his doings. But they who have evil designs in their hearts bring upon themselves death and captivity, especially those who obtain this world for themselves, and glory in their wealth, and do not lay hold of the good things which are to come.

The apocalyptic perspective of the angelic promise and threat is evident in the wording of the citation. "The good things which are to come" refers to the heavenly treasure that was commonly held by Christians to be stored for them until the day of judgment (see 1 Peter 1:3–5).

The apocalyptic convictions of *The Shepherd of Hermas* are evident and amply support the scholarly reading of the document that has become a matter of consensus. But it is equally apparent that there is another sort of conviction at work. Hermas is assured that the righteous "finds the Lord ready to assist him in all his doings." The promise, that is, is for support in the present, not only in the final judgment that is to come. Similarly, the fate of the wicked is "death and captivity" and not a purely eschatological threat.

The social setting of *The Shepherd of Hermas* makes the promise and the threat all the more striking. On the basis of earlier materials, "Hermas" finally composed *The Shepherd* around the year 150 C.E., just when intellectuals reached a crescendo in their attacks on Christians. Fronto, tutor of the emperors Antoninus and Marcus Aurelius (and consul under Hadrian), charged that Christians worshiped an ass's head, sacrificed children, and encouraged promiscuity during worship.⁹ Under such circumstances, to imagine oneself as assisted and punished by the Lord takes on a particular meaning.

The righteous who "finds the Lord ready to assist him in all his doings" discovers support, then, in the midst of suspicion, but not so much prosperity that he becomes one of those who "obtain this world for themselves, and glory in their wealth." Just as Christians attempted to walk a fine line between the Roman hostility that would destroy their lives and the accommodation to Rome that would destroy their souls, so Hermas is called to a life of just getting along with divine support. In that position, he is to escape both the wrath of God and death at the hands of Caesar.

*The Shepherd of Hermas* is often written off as a product of "no great intelligence."¹⁰ That evaluation is framed in intellectual and literary terms in comparison with the vigorous theology of other Christian works of the second century (such as those of Justin Martyr, Irenaeus, Tertullian, and Clement of Alexandria). But *The Shepherd* should be evaluated within the social function in Rome that it evidently performed, and performed to such good effect that it was actively discussed whether the work belonged within the New Testament. *The Shepherd* elaborates and develops the recommendation for the social posture of disciples that is already evident in the Gospel According to Mark (from the first century).

Mark's ending has long caused perplexity, because the Gospel closes with the women at the tomb, having been told of the resurrection of Jesus, departing in silence, "for they were afraid" (16:8). Longer endings were later added to Mark to make it accord better with the other Gospels, but the emphatic silence of the women was clearly intended as the final image of the original work. Such silence is only perplexing, however, when Mark is read outside the context of the recent and vicious persecution instituted by Nero in 64 C.E. Within that setting, Mark is recommending a rational policy: discipleship with a low profile. The women are to know what they know, but not to spread their knowledge abroad indiscriminately.

The position of Christians in Rome by the time of *The Shepherd of Hermas* is less fraught with immediate danger but still precarious. Hermas describes himself as a freed slave who had acquired family and property. His own precarious situation, then, is defined as in between the unstable policy of Rome and the absolute requirements of God. The only acceptable position is to be assisted by the Lord in one's living (on the one hand), but (on the other hand) also not to permit even this divine assistance to turn into a love of wealth. The Markan motif of low-profile discipleship becomes in *The Shepherd of Hermas* a complete program of how to realize that aim in a hostile environment.

Hermas lays out his chief concern as the problem of sin. Given that, as he is told, the righteous are only as righteous as their intentions, Hermas panics, "If this sin is recorded against me, how shall I be saved?" (*Shepherd* I.2.1). In another vision, the grounds of his fear are only confirmed. A great and old woman appears, seated on a throne of snow white wool. That description echoes the appearance of God himself in the vision of Daniel 7:9, and Hermas is eventually told that the venerable matron is the Church (*Shepherd* II.4.1). It is she who underscores what Hermas has already learned (*Shepherd* I.2.4): "For it is an evil and mad purpose against a revered spirit and one already approved, if a man desire an evil deed, and especially if it be Hermas the temperate, who abstains from every evil desire and is full of all simplicity and great innocence." The authority of the church, then, only reinforces the desperate predicament of all who are like Hermas. Because the issue is one's intentions and desires, not only one's actions, the problem seems here to be set up as impossible to solve. And in that the issue is the lack of complete control over what he thinks, Hermas's predicament seems to be universal.

*The Shepherd of Hermas* here identifies, with the greatest precision of any extant document from the early church, how the problem of sin was seen to threaten the integrity of the faith overall. As compared to the social issue of how to conduct oneself as a disciple in an inhospitable environment, the deeper incongruity of being held responsible for whatever one might think and feel was a far more fundamental problem. After all, that concern could feed the response of a dualistic Gnosticism,[11] which would make the nature of one's desire a symptom of whether one was spiritual in one's constitution. A counsel of despair is an obvious response to the command to control one's desire. If Hermas must determine his desires in order to be saved, the most rational course might be to admit that he is not saved and cannot be.

*The Shepherd of Hermas* resolves the dilemma in what the angelic representation of the church goes on to say. God's anger for evil intents is confirmed, but the grounds of his anger are said to be other than the issue of intents (*Shepherd* I.3.1): "But it is not for this that God is angry with you, but in order that you should convert your family, which has sinned against the Lord, and against you, their parents." The answer to the dilemma of human intention is given: it is the mercy of divine restraint. Although God would justly be angered by the failure of good intent among the righteous, he is compassionate enough to provide a remedy. If at least they will see to the nurture of their families, he will not be angry.

The symmetry of God's willingness to accept the nurture of one's family in the place of intentional perfection is simply stated. In the social realm, one can act with greater conscious control than in the purely personal realm (*Shepherd* I.3.2): "For as the smith, by hammering his work, overcomes the task which he desires, so also the daily righteous word overcomes all wickedness." The *Shepherd* comes to a confidence in reasoned behavior, as influenced by the "Word" of God, which corresponds to Clement of Alexandria's much more philosophical theology of Christ, also developed in the second century.[12]

Clement's approach was inventive, and a continuation of the identification between Jesus and the Word of God made in the Gospel According to John (1:1–18) and by Justin Martyr (another second-century thinker). Clement insisted that the Word was influential even in one's passions. But Clement's thought, *The Shepherd* shows us, is also representative of popular Christian belief. The "daily righteous word" of God, God's accessibility through reason and speech and deliberate action, was widely understood to "overcome all wickedness," whether in the world or in one's heart.

The family is a vital sphere of Christian action in *The Shepherd of Hermas* because it is the one place where it is assumed Hermas exerts influence. "The affairs of daily life" in the world are assumed to corrupt families, and Hermas is instructed to correct his own family, especially his children (*Shepherd* I.3.1–2). Later, the same principle will include Hermas's wife within his family, and it will be extended to the church at large (*Shepherd* II.2).

The placement of the family as at the center of action marks a signal development in Christian theology. The position attributed to Jesus in the primitive church envisaged the renunciation of family for the sake of the Gospel (see Matt. 19:27–30; Mark 10:28–31; Luke 18:28–30). That position was modulated within early Christianity as represented by the New Testament: the relationships of family were portrayed as providing an opportunity for enacting the love one had learned in Christ (see 1 Peter 2:18–3:7).

By the time of *The Shepherd of Hermas*, however, a deeper transformation in the evaluation of family had occurred. It was now the sphere of first recourse in working out one's constitutional inability to offer God the perfection he required. Here, in fact, is the source of the vital concern for family within classical Christianity. It is not merely a "value" or a place of affection: family is where salvation is ordinarily worked out.

The imperative to Christian leaders sums up the ethical perspective on salvation that is developed in *The Shepherd of Hermas* (II.2.7): "You, therefore, who do righteousness, remain steadfast and do not be double-minded, that your way might be with the angels." By this point in the book it has already been shown that an individual cannot avoid being double-minded to some extent: aspects of the imagination simply evade complete control. But one can be dedicated to the rational, deliberate task of nurturing one's family and the family of the church: that is what God demands by way of repentance.

A remarkable tension has been evident within Christianity from the time of its classical formulations during the course of the second century. On the one hand, family and sexual relations have been viewed as pertaining to a condition of flesh that is to be overcome; on the other hand, such relationships have been held up as the normative field within which salvation may be worked out.

*The Shepherd of Hermas*, precisely because it is a relatively unsophisticated document, represents this tension quite clearly (II.2.3): "But make these words known to all your children and to your wife, who shall in future be to you as a sister. For she does not refrain her tongue, with which she sins; but when she has heard these words she will refrain it, and will obtain mercy." Sexual relations are blandly put aside when they are implicitly typified as incestuous (relations with a "sister"). By contrast, inappropriate speech is given labored attention. Christianity constructed for itself the image of the perfect woman, obedient, celibate (except for the imperative for motherhood), and silent, because it located the struggle for salvation within social and human terms.

Making flesh the vessel of spirit inevitably meant that the flesh was neither embraced nor denied as it is, but changed.

Wives become "sisters" as certainly as people become angelic in the resurrection (see Matt. 22:30; Mark 12:25; Luke 20:36). The perspective of Jesus had emphasized that transformation, but without insisting that people *in their flesh* would become like angels. In its struggle with Gnosticism during the second century, the faith that came to be known as orthodox embraced the flesh as an ultimate concern in a way that had not been the case earlier.

## DEVIATIONS FROM THE IDEAL

Augustine of Hippo (354–430 C.E.) is featured in our discussion of Christianity in *God* and *Evil and Suffering*, two other volumes in the Pilgrim Library of World Religions series. He is a pivotal figure, to some extent because he lived during a time of severe trial for Christianity, in certain ways as severe as the persecution of the time before Constantine.

In 410 C.E., Alaric sacked the city of Rome itself. That event was a stunning blow to the empire generally, but it was a double blow to Latin Christianity. First, the pillage occurred while the empire was Christian; two centuries before, Tertullian had argued that idolatry brought about disaster (see *Apologeticus* 41.1), and now Christianity could be said to do so. Second, Latin Christianity—especially in North Africa—had been particularly attracted to a millenarian eschatology. How could one explain that the triumphant end of history, announced by Eusebius and his followers in connection with Constantine's accession to power, seemed to be reversed by the Goths?

The explanation of that dilemma occupied Augustine in his *City of God*, a tremendous work of twenty-three books written between 413 and 426. From the outset, he sounds his theme, that the City of God is an eternal city that exists in the midst of the cities of men; those two cities are both mixed and at odds in this world, but they are to be separated by the final judgment (*City of God* 1.1). That essentially simple thesis is sustained through an account of Roman religion and Hellenistic philosophy, including Augustine's critical appreciation of Plato (books 1–10).

In the central section of his work Augustine sets out his case within a discussion of truly global history from the story of the creation in Genesis. From the fall of the angels, which Augustine associates with the separation of light and darkness in Genesis 1:4, he speaks of the striving between good and evil. But the distinction between those two is involved with the *will* of certain angels, not with any intrinsic wickedness (*City of God* 11.33). People, too, are disordered in their desire, rather than in their creation by God (*City of God* 12.8).

The difference between the will God intends for his creatures and the will they actually evince attests the freedom involved in divine creation. But the effect of perverted will, whether angelic or human, is to establish two antithetical regimes (*City of God* 14.28):

> So two loves have constituted two cities—the earthly is formed by love of self even to contempt of God, the heavenly by love of God even to contempt of self. For the one glories in herself, the other in the Lord. The one seeks glory from man; for the other God, the witness of the conscience, is the greatest glory. . . . In the one the lust for power prevails, both in her own rulers and in the nations she subdues; in the other all serve each other in charity, governors by taking thought for all and subjects by obeying.

By book 18, Augustine arrives at his own time and repeats that the two cities "alike enjoy temporal goods or suffer temporal ills, but differ in faith, in hope, in love, until they be separated by the final judgment and each receives its end, of which there is no end" (*City of God* 18.54).

That commits Augustine to speak of eschatological issues, which he does until the end of the work as a whole. Given what we found in our discussion in *Evil and Suffering*, that is not surprising: Christianity's commitment to the creation as God's work inevitably involves the hope of the transcendence of evil. It is in his discussion of eschatology that Augustine frames classic and orthodox responses to some of the most persistent questions of the Christian theology of his time. He adheres to the expectation of the resurrection of the flesh, not simply of the body (as had been the manner of Origen during the third century). In so doing, he refutes the Manichaean philosophy he accepted prior to his conversion to Christianity. In Manichaeanism, named after a Persian teacher of the third century called Mani, light and darkness are two eternal substances that struggle against one another, and they war over the creation they have both participated in making. As in the case of Gnosticism, on which it was dependent, Manichaeanism counseled a denial of the flesh. By his insistence on the resurrection of the flesh, Augustine revives the strong assertion of the extent of God's embrace of his own creation in the tradition of Latin Christianity.

Because Augustine was committed to an insistence on the resurrection of the flesh, he had to respond to criticism (*City of God* 22.12):

> Some question us very closely, and in their questioning ridicule our belief in the resurrected flesh. They ask whether abortive fetuses will rise again; they quote the words of the Lord: "Truly I say unto you, not a hair of your head shall perish," and then ask whether all will have equal height and strength, or will have different bodily sizes. For if the size of all bodies is to be equal, how will those abortive births (if they, too, are to rise again) have a bodily size that they did not have before? Or, if they are not to rise, since they were not properly born, but discharged, the same question is raised of infants—when they die in infancy, how will they acquire the stature that we now see is lacking? For we will not deny the

resurrection of any who are capable of both being born, and of being born again in baptism. Then they ask how that equality is to be accommodated. For if all are to be as large and as tall as the largest and tallest have been here, the problem concerns not only infants, but also the majority of men: from what source will come the portion that was lacking here, if each one is to receive what he had here?

Augustine shows no liking for such questions, but at the same time he clearly indicates that there was disagreement and ferment within the church of his period in coming to grips with issues of life after death. (That lively controversy and inquiry will especially concern us in *Death and the Afterlife*, the final volume in the Pilgrim Library of World Religions series.)

For the moment, what is immediately pertinent to our theme is that Augustine is required by the logic of his own argument to confront the particular issue of sexual differences between people. That is just what he does later in the same passage (*City of God* 22.17):

> Because it is said, "Until we all come to the perfect man, to the measure of the stature of the fullness of Christ," and "Conformed to the image of the son of God," some believe that women will not rise in female sex, but that all will be males, since God made only man from clay, and the woman from the man. But they seem wiser to me who do not doubt that both sexes will rise. For there will be no lust there, which is the cause of shame. For before they sinned they were naked, and the man and the woman were not ashamed. So all defects will be taken away from those bodies, but their nature will be preserved. The female sex is not a defect, but a natural state, which will then be free from intercourse and childbirth. There will be female parts, not suited to their old use, but to a new beauty, and this will not arouse the greed of the beholder,

for there will be no greed, but it will inspire praise of the wisdom and goodness of God, who both created what was not, and freed from corruption what he made.

The objection raised to Augustine's position is on the basis of Genesis 2, where the primordial man and woman are made, and he replies by means of the same passage. His assumption, following the line of his *City of God* as a whole, is that the depiction of the Fall of humanity as a result of love of self can be reversed to understand how the love of God will transform us.

Part of that transformation, in Augustine's vision, is to include male and female, no longer as instruments of intercourse and childbirth, but as in the image of God, created male and female (so Genesis 1:27).[13] Throughout, it is plain that Augustine casts human sexuality as a problem, beset by the corruption of greed (the debased product of self-love). For that reason, writing as a male, he casts the problem as a whole as that of men wanting women for their own use, and he acknowledges his personal difficulty in just that regard (in *City of God* 22.22). That particular association of females with sexuality is typical of Late Antiquity, and is especially prominent in Gnostic writings, where women's desire to be as creative as men leads them to literally hysterical reproduction (see, for example, *On the Origin of the World*).[14] What is crucial in Augustine's analysis, however, is the simple and revolutionary statement, "The female sex is not a defect, but a natural state." That denies that femininity is to be described as the privation of the masculine, but must rather be seen as engendered by God as part of creation and not simply for the practicalities of reproduction.

That is, Augustine imagines gender, which is engendered by God in God's image, as distinct from sexuality, a characteristic of the corrupt state of humanity. In order to do so, he needs to address the interpretation of a famous teaching of Jesus in which people in the resurrection are compared to angels, neither marrying nor being given in marriage (see Matt. 22:30; Mark 12:25; Luke 20:35–36). Augustine explains this passage in *City of God* 22.18:

> They will be equal to angels in immortality and happiness, not in flesh, nor indeed in resurrection, which the angels had no need of, since they could not die. So the Lord said that there would be no marriage in the resurrection, not that there would be no women. And at the time a question was under consideration that he could have settled more quickly and easily by denying the female sex, if he had foreknown that there was to be none. Instead, he proved that there would be when he said: "They will not marry," which is said of women, "nor take wives," which is said of men. So those who either marry husbands or take wives here will be present there, but will not do those things there.

So, for Augustine, people are raised with their created, natural gender and are raised sufficiently recognizably that they are present to one another in the resurrection as engendered.

In his adherence to a kind of millenarianism and to the resurrection of the flesh in the Latin creed, Augustine is very much a product of North Africa and Italy, where he was active (chiefly as a teacher of rhetoric) prior to his conversion and his return to North Africa. But his *City of God* creates the greater frame, primordial and eschatological, within which history becomes a theological discipline. Here, he argues, is more than a lesson in how to avoid war and create order. And here there is certainly more than the superficial enthusiasm that comes of histories written by the winners. Rather, history for Augustine—and from Augustine—is the interplay of those two forces that determine the existence of every society, every person.

The struggle, however, is not ultimately between good and

evil but between the love of God and the love of self. That is the key to Augustine's ceaseless, pastoral ministry, as well as to his remarkably broad intellectual horizon. In every time and in every place, there is the possibility that the City of God will be revealed and embraced; now, in the church, we at last know its name and can see the face of that love that would transform us all. Part of that transformation is the insight that female and male are not only sexual roles but two sides of engendered humanity in the image of God. The family in its present constitution has also been replaced as the field within which God's love is worked out in human terms. Instead, the City of God is understood to be that which offers the possibility in any place of recognizing in one another the sisters and brothers of Christ.

## WOMEN AND PUBLIC LIFE

In the period since the end of the Second World War, feminism has been among the most important influences within the development of Christianity. Feminists have revolutionized both the self-understandings of women and men and the critical appreciation of the sources of Christianity. By way of definition, we consider feminism here as the effort to evaluate femininity within its own terms of reference and not merely as a function of sexual utility or attraction.

A good description of feminist interpretation as widely practiced is offered in a recent book, a collaborative effort edited by Elisabeth Schüssler Fiorenza and others:

> Rather than focusing only on the women's passages, it generally seeks to analyze writings in their entirety. This method is used in order to assess how much the texts religiously advocate and foster all women's and marginalized men's subordination and exploitation and how much they transgress the kyriarchal boundaries of their time.[15]

The adjective *kyriarchal* is derived from the Greek *kurios,* which means "lord." The concern here is with a lordship of dominance and a dynamic of what Schüssler Fiorenza calls transgression, but which might more naturally be described as liberation, as she goes on to explain:

> Its contributors "search the scriptures" in a double sense. They scrutinize and interrogate the scriptures to uncover their "crimes" of silencing and marginalization. Moreover, most of them also seek to bring to the fore and make audible again the subjugated voices and suppressed traditions that have left traces in ancient writings.[16]

The assumption in such work is that what has been subjugated and suppressed in the past might instruct us, that it is coherent enough to provide alternatives, and in some sense better alternatives, to the dominant emphasis of the lords of this world and of Christianity.

The emphasis upon the evaluation of documents in their entirety is in fact characteristic of feminist concerns, because context has long been a characteristic concern within feminism. Only within her context can one evaluate a person and assess the degrees to which she might be exploited and/or empowered to express who she is. When that insight is applied to texts, the result is to resist the atomizing of passages, which has been characteristic of conventional scholarship. Instead, one tends to seek the meaning of wholes, and of wholes in relation to one another. It is no coincidence that the period of the influence of feminism has also evidenced a greater interest in the social contexts of Christianity.

In the same volume Schüssler Fiorenza edited, Turid Karlsen Seim analyzes just the passage in Luke's Gospel (10:38–42) that was introduced at the beginning of this essay. In a sensitive reading, she emphasizes that empowerment or liberation is the focus:

> Mary sitting at the Lord's feet and listening to his words is portrayed in the typical position of the pupil (cf. Acts 22:3). This description of a teacher-pupil relationship is an important feature of the text. The role as student in which Mary is positioned goes beyond the normal opportunity for women to hear the word in the context of worship. Moreover, the text alludes to terms that in rabbinic tradition are connected to teaching institutions. It also echoes other sayings about "hearing the word" as the decisive criterion for discipleship directed to both women and men (see Luke 6:46 ff.; 8:15, 21; 11:28).[17]

But alongside this liberating tendency of the text, Seim also explores what she calls the "passivity and silence" of Mary. After all, she merely listens, and Martha does not even speak to her, but to Jesus. While men who listen "may become public preachers, women are never given any explicit commission to preach."[18]

What increased attention to context has enabled Seim to do is expose the ambivalence of Luke's Gospel in its presentation of women. She also refers to Acts in this regard, which was written as a sequel to follow Luke (see Acts 1:1–5), and that strengthens her analysis. But in that regard, there is a connection she does not make that proves interesting. In Acts 6, the apostles are portrayed as refusing "to abandon the word of the Lord and serve tables" (6:2). That is what prompts them to appoint "servants" (*diakonoi*, "deacons"), who administer nourishment to the community while the apostles continue in prayer and the service of the Word (see Acts 6:1–6).

Seim is helpful in calling attention to the absence of any explicit authorization that Mary should preach, but it is also appropriate to observe the resonance of Mary with the place of the apostles. Her silence is not well characterized as a mere matter of passivity, because she demonstrates the continuing attendance to the Word which even the apostles were momentarily distracted from. Her "good part" is not merely to be like the apostles, but to be better than they in her constant commitment to the Word. That creates a tension in Luke-Acts: women are indeed assigned places, and on the whole they are well described as marginalized, but at the same time the positive but partial correspondence between what women do and what fully empowered men do invites a development beyond the text. In just that sense, feminist interpretation may legitimately claim to speak of what texts are pointing to more faithfully than other forms of interpretation.

## CONCLUSION

At first, the variety of Christian models of gender and familial relationship may seem bewildering. But the four distinctive models we have considered in fact relate to each other closely. Feminist confidence that gender is contextual, and to be assessed contextually in regard to its repression and liberation, is not based on an objective standard of truth, but on conviction. That conviction is that gender is not merely functional or instrumental, whether for reproduction or for pleasure. Rather, gender is understood to be engendered, part of the meaningful configuration of humanity as shaped by God, which includes relationships that become "family" only in the metaphorical sense of which Jesus spoke. In that sense, feminist interpretation develops naturally from the analysis of Augustine.

But Augustine, of course, worked in no vacuum. The bold conviction of *The Shepherd of Hermas* may seem to be rudely expressed as compared to the vast learning and elegant exposition of *City of God*, but those two works share the confidence that how people relate to one another in social terms represents and develops how they relate to God. Whether it is a question of family or of society, how we behave toward our neighbor is the measure of how God engages us (see also Matt. 25:31–46). And that is true only because the insight of Jesus is taken to be axiomatic: if God is our truest parent, then our relations need continually to be worked out as sisters and brothers.

Sisters and brothers are related throughout life and beyond life. Their genders, along with many other elements, are naturally a part of them, and yet they relate to one another, not sexually first of all, but as different members of the same family. Christian attitudes toward gender and family, and even Christian definitions of what those are, have varied quite widely. But throughout there is an underlying coherence. Our most powerful and significant relationship is with God, our common parent. That, for every Christian and for all Christians, is the fully engaged relationship from which meaning is generated. We know who we are, become what we are, understand how we are to be in relation to God. But all that is for the most part understood not in the abstract realm, but in how we engage with other children of God. Within that family, relationships are engendered in which we find our gender, our truest expression of the natures given us in creation.

CHAPTER 3

# *Judaism*

What a rare find is a capable wife!
Her worth is far beyond that of rubies.
Her husband puts his confidence in her
and lacks no good thing.
She is good to him, never bad,
All the days of her life.
She looks for wool and flax,
And sets her hand to them with a will.
She is like a merchant fleet,
Bringing her food from afar.
She rises while it is still night,
And supplies provisions for her household,
The daily fare of her maids.
She sets her mind on an estate and acquires it;
She plants a vineyard by her own labors.
She girds herself with strength,
And performs her tasks with vigor.
She sees that her business thrives;
Her lamp never goes out at night.
She sets her hand to the distaff;
Her fingers work the spindle.
She gives generously to the poor;
Her hands are stretched out to the needy.
She is not worried for her household because of snow,

For her household is dressed in crimson.
She makes covers for herself;
Her clothing is linen and purple.
Her husband is prominent in the gates,
As he sits among the elders of the land.
She makes cloth and sells it,
And offers a girdle to the merchant.
She is clothed with strength and splendor;
She looks to the future cheerfully.
Her mouth is full of wisdom,
Her tongue with kindly teaching.
She oversees the activities of her household
And never eats the bread of idleness.
Her children declare her happy;
Her husband praises her,
"Many Women have done well,
But you surpass them all."
Grace is deceptive,
Beauty is illusory;
It is for her fear of the Lord
That a woman is to be praised.
Extol her for the fruit of her hand,
And let her works praise her in the gates.

—Proverbs 31:10–31[1]

## MODELS OF VIRTUE FOR WOMEN THROUGH THE LIFE CYCLE

Recited at the dinner table on the Sabbath evening, Friday night, by a husband to his wife in the presence of the family, the hymn of praise defines the Judaic model of virtue for women: sturdy, autonomous, charged with unique and critical tasks, principal and full partner in the venture of life, which is to form a family and raise children in the Torah. As we shall see, moreover, the virtues of women extend to those of heart as well as hearth, with the result that correct attitudes as much as proper actions derive from feminine models and are assigned to men as much as to women for emulation. Judaism in its classical documents, therefore, may be characterized as thoroughly androgynous; that is, joining traits explicitly marked as male to those explicitly classified as female and insisting upon both in the formation of models of virtue. All Israel is to emulate women's virtue, the condition of the coming of the Messiah. And women's capacity for devotion, selfless faith, and loyalty defines the model of what is required of Israel for its virtue.

To understand the position of women within the religious system of Judaism in its classical sources, we must realize that sages thought in terms of the holy community, not in terms of isolated individuals. Gender roles formed part of the larger statement that sages proposed to craft concerning the coherent life of the community overall. Sages' doctrine of feminine virtue, therefore, makes sense only within its larger systemic context. The dual Torah, beginning to end, taught that the Israelite was to exhibit the moral virtues of subservience, patience, endurance, and hope. These would translate into the emotional traits of humility and forbearance. And they would yield to social virtues of passivity and conciliation. The hero was one who overcame impulses, and the truly virtuous person, the one who reconciled others by giving way before the opinions of others. All of these acts of self-abnegation and self-denial, accommodation rather than rebellion, are required to begin with the right attitudes, sentiments, emotions, and impulses, and the single most dominant motif of the Rabbinic writings, start to finish, is its stress on the right attitudes leading to the right action, the correct intentionalities producing the besought decision, and, above all, accommodating in one's heart to what could not be changed by one's action. And that meant the world as it was. Sages prepared Israel for the long centuries of subordination and alienation by inculcating attitudes that best suited people who could govern little more than how they felt about things. As we shall now see, sages themselves classified the besought virtues as feminine, and they proposed to feminize Israel, the holy people.

When we speak of virtues as feminine and masculine, it is not to perpetuate contemporary stereotypes but to pay close attention to sages' own judgment of matters. How do we know how the framers of the dual Torah, who bear the title "our sages of blessed memory," classify virtues, whether as masculine or as feminine? In the classical writings we have several systematic exegeses that focus on women and therefore permit us to characterize sages' conception of women's virtues and, it will follow, the virtues they classify as feminine. Sages' reading of the Scriptural books of Ruth and Esther and their treatment of Miriam the prophetess and other scriptural prophetesses allow access to their thinking on what characterizes the virtuous woman—her alone.

Among the expositions pertinent to that matter, however, none more reliably records sages' conception of the feminine and of the feminine in relationship to the masculine than their reading of the Song of Songs in the exegetical compilation, Song of Songs Rabbah, a writing contemporary with the Talmud of Babylonia, circa 600. There, in reading the Song of Songs as a statement of the relationship of God and Israel, Israel is identified as the female beloved, God as the male lover. We need not speculate, therefore, on correct traits for women; in the document at hand, they are those explicitly assigned to feminine Israel. So we now turn to a brief survey of what is said in so many words. Because of the critical place of Song of Songs Rabbah in the representation of androgynous Judaism and, in particular, the definition of the feminine component of the androgyneity, I cite representative passages at considerable length.

The first point is the most telling. The relationship of Israel to God is the same as the relationship of a wife to the husband, and this is explicit in the following:

> I am my beloved's, and his desire is for me.
> "I am my beloved's, and his desire is for me:"
> There are three yearnings:
> The yearning of Israel is only for their Father who is in heaven, as it is said, "I am my beloved's, and his desire is for me."
> The yearning of a woman is only for her husband: "And your desire shall be for your husband" (Gen. 3:16).
> The yearning of the Evil Impulse is only for Cain and his ilk: "To you is its desire" (Gen. 4:7).
> —Song of Songs Rabbah to Song 7:10

Here, therefore, we find that gender relationships are explicitly characterized and, with them, the traits associated with the genders as well.

Our sages turn to everyday experience—the love of husband and wife—for a metaphor for God's love for Israel and Israel's love for God. And Israel is assigned the feminine role and the feminine virtues. It is difficult to identify a more extravagant form of praise for women's virtue, her capacity to love generously and in an act of unearned grace. Then, when Solomon's song says, "O that you would kiss me with the kisses of your mouth! For your love is better than wine" (Song 1:2), sages of blessed memory think of how God kissed Israel. Reading the Song of Songs as a metaphor, the Judaic sages as a matter of fact state in a systematic and orderly way their entire structure and system and, along the way, permit us to identify the traits they associate with feminine Israel and masculine God, respectively.

What is important here, however, is not the document's doctrinal message but its implicit and tacit affirmations. The document does not set forth a great many explicit doctrines but delivers its message through the description of attitudes and emotions. And our particular interest lies in the identification of the systems designative as feminine and masculine of clearly defined attitudes and emotions. The writers mean to paint word pictures, evoke feelings, speak empathetically rather than only sympathetically. Song of Songs Rabbah tells how to think and feel, forming sensibility in the formation of the heart at one with God.

No account of feminine virtue can accomplish its goals without cataloging masculine virtue as well. Our survey of the feminine and the masculine in Song of Songs Rabbah begins with the clear characterization of God as masculine, Israel as feminine:

> My beloved has gone down to his garden, to the beds of spices, to pasture his flock in the gardens, and to gather lilies.
>
> "My beloved has gone down to his garden, to the beds of spices, [to pasture his flock in the gardens, and to gather lilies]:"
>
> Said R. Yosé b. R. Hanina, "As to this verse, the beginning of it is not the same as the end, and the end not the same as the beginning.
>
> "The verse had only to say, 'My beloved has gone down to pasture in his garden,' but you say, 'in the gardens'!
>
> "But 'my beloved' is the Holy One, blessed be he;
>
> "'to his garden' refers to the world.
>
> "'to the beds of spices' refers to Israel.
>
> "'to pasture his flock in the gardens' refers to synagogues and school-houses.
>
> "'and to gather lilies' speaks of picking [taking away in death] the righteous that are in Israel."
>
> —Song of Songs Rabbah to Song 6:2

"My beloved" is God; the choice part of the garden, which is the world, is Israel, its synagogues and houses of study. Israel is now the faithful beloved, waiting patiently for her lover, always trusting in His faithfulness.

> Set me as a seal upon your heart, as a seal upon your arm; for love is strong as death, jealousy is cruel as the grave. Its flashes are flashes of fire, a most vehement flame.
>
> "for love is strong as death:"
> As strong as death is the love with which the Holy One, blessed be he, loves Israel: "I have loved you says the Lord" (Mal. 1:2).
> "jealousy is cruel as the grave:"
> That is when they make him jealous with their idolatry: "They roused him to jealousy with strange gods" (Dt. 32:16).
> Another explanation of "for love is strong as death:"
> As strong as death is the love with which a man loves his wife: "Enjoy life with the wife whom you love" (Qoh. 9:9).
> "jealousy is cruel as the grave:"
> the jealousy that she causes in him and leads him to say to her, "Do not speak with such-and-so."
> If she goes and speaks with that man, forthwith: "The spirit of jealousy comes upon him and he is jealous on account of his wife" (Num. 5:14).
>
> —Song of Songs Rabbah to Song 8:6

Israel's feminine character is now well established, and the ways in which the exegesis of the song is worked out in response to that fact are clear. Then we have to ask ourselves, precisely what kind of relationship does feminine Israel have with the masculine God? The answer is, the relationship of a wife to a husband.

Israel's status as God's beloved yields two important results. First, the metaphor is treated as neuter, in that, even though Israel is feminine, that fact bears no material consequence for the representation of Israel. The repertoire of word symbols that convey the principal components of the structure of faith is set forth in terms of what is simply a useful metaphor. But the metaphor is not realized, for example, in the formulation of traits set forth as unique to women and unique to feminine Israel by reason of its femininity. Representative of many passages, the following suffices to show how, despite the femininity of Israel, the framers are able to run through the principal elements of Israel's sacred history—Egypt, the Sea, Sinai, the subjugation to the kingdoms but the coming redemption by reason of Israel's faithfulness to the covenant:

> I am a rose of Sharon, a lily of the valleys.
> "I am a rose of Sharon, [a lily of the valleys]:"
> Said the Community of Israel, "I am the one, and I am beloved.
> "I am the one whom the Holy One, blessed be he, loved more than the seventy nations."
> "I am a rose of Sharon:"
> "For I made for him a shade through Bezalel [the words for shade and Bezalel use the same consonants as the word for rose]: 'And Bezalel made the ark' (Ex. 38:1)."
> "of Sharon:"
> "For I said before him a song [which word uses the same consonants as the word for Sharon] through Moses:
> "'Then sang Moses and the children of Israel' (Ex. 15:1)."

Another explanation of the phrase, "I am a rose of Sharon":

> Said the Community of Israel, "I am the one, and I am beloved.
> "I am the one who was hidden in the shadow of Egypt, but in a brief moment the Holy One, blessed be he, brought me together to Raamses, and I blossomed forth in good deeds like a rose, and I said before him this song: 'You shall have a song as in the night when a feast is sanctified' (Is. 30:29)."

Another explanation of the phrase, "I am a rose of Sharon":

> Said the Community of Israel, "I am the one, and I am beloved.
> "I am the one who was hidden in the shadow of the sea, but in a brief moment I blossomed forth in good deeds like a rose, and I pointed to him with the finger (opposite to me): 'This is my God and I will glorify him' (Ex. 15:2)."

Another explanation of the phrase, "I am a rose of Sharon":

> Said the Community of Israel, "I am the one, and I am beloved.
> "I am the one who was hidden in the shadow of Mount Sinai, but in a brief moment I blossomed forth in good deeds like a lily in hand and in heart, and I said before him, 'All that the Lord has said we will do and obey' (Ex. 24:7)."

Another explanation of the phrase, "I am a rose of Sharon":

> Said the Community of Israel, "I am the one, and I am beloved.
> "I am the one who was hidden and downtrodden in the shadow of the kingdoms. But tomorrow, when the Holy One, blessed be he, redeems me from the shadow of the kingdoms, I shall blossom forth like a lily and say before him a new song: 'Sing to the Lord a new song, for he has done marvelous things, his right hand and his holy arm have wrought salvation for him' (Ps. 98:1)."
> —Song of Songs Rabbah to Song 2:1

To make the point that its author wishes to register, the foregoing passage does not require that Israel be represented as feminine. Nor do traits identified with femininity emerge. What we have is simply a review of standard high points in sages' theology of Israel's history: Egypt, the Sea, Sinai, then the whole of the intervening history homogenized into the single, dreadful time of subjugation to the kingdoms, and, finally, redemption, to which we shall return at the end of this chapter.

The virtues of wives, portrayed as feminine, once more are those of loyalty and submission. This metaphor is exploited through the invocation of the wife's trust in the husband, the mark of the perfect wife. Israel follows wherever Moses, in behalf of God, leads; Israel trusts in God the way a woman who has accepted marriage trusts her husband:

> R. Berekhiah in the name of R. Judah b. R. Ilai: "It is written, 'And Moses led Israel onward from the Red Sea' (Ex. 15:22):
>
> "He led them on from the sin committed at the sea.
>
> "They said to him, 'Moses, our lord, where are you leading us?'
>
> "He said to them, 'To Elim, from Elim to Alush, from Alush to Marah, from Marah to Rephidim, from Rephidim to Sinai.'
>
> "They said to him, 'Indeed, wherever you go and lead us, we are with you.'
>
> "The matter is comparable to the case of one who went and married a woman from a village. He said to her, 'Arise and come with me.'
>
> "She said to him, 'From here to where?'
>
> "He said to her, 'From here to Tiberias, from Tiberias to the Tannery, from the Tannery to the Upper Market, from the Upper Market to the Lower Market.'
>
> "She said to him, 'Wherever you go and take me, I shall go with you.'
>
> "So said the Israelites, 'My soul cleaves to you' (Ps. 63:9)."
>
> —Song of Songs Rabbah to Song 4:12

Israel's feminine virtue must exceed even the wife's trust in the husband's protection. Israel also must care only for God, the way a wife's entire desire is solely for her husband. The point is unmistakable and critical. Israel is subject to an oath to wait patiently for God's redemption, not to rebel against the nations on its own; that is the concrete social politics meant to derive from the analogy of Israel's relationship to God to the wife's relationship to the husband: perfect submission, and also perfect trust. Rebellion against the nations stands for arrogance on Israel's part, an act of lack of trust and therefore lack of faithfulness. Implicit in this representation of the right relationship, of course, is the promise that feminine Israel will evoke from the masculine God the response of commitment and intervention: God will intervene to save Israel, when Israel makes herself into the perfect wife of God.

The upshot is, Israel must fulfill the vocation of a woman, turn itself into a woman, serve God as a wife serves a husband. The question then follows: is it possible that the Judaism that has treated the present document as canonical asks men to turn themselves into women? And the answer is, that demand is stated in so many words. Here we find a full statement of the feminization of the masculine. The two brothers, Moses and Aaron, are compared to Israel's breasts, a reversal of gender classifications that can hardly be more extreme or dramatic:

> Your two breasts are like two fawns, twins of a gazelle, that feed among the lilies.
> 
> "Your two breasts are like two fawns:"
> 
> this refers to Moses and Aaron.
> 
> Just as a woman's breasts are her glory and her ornament,
> 
> so Moses and Aaron are the glory and the ornament of Israel.
> 
> Just as a woman's breasts are her charm, so Moses and Aaron are the charm of Israel.
> 
> Just as a woman's breasts are her honor and her praise, so Moses and Aaron are the honor and praise of Israel.
> 
> Just as a woman's breasts are full of milk, so Moses and Aaron are full of Torah.
> 
> Just as whatever a woman eats the infant eats and sucks, so all

the Torah that our lord, Moses, learned he taught to Aaron: "And Moses told Aaron all the words of the Lord" (Ex. 4:28).

And rabbis say, "He actually revealed the Ineffable Name of God to him."

Just as one breast is not larger than the other, so Moses and Aaron were the same: "These are Moses and Aaron" (Ex. 6:27), "These are Aaron and Moses" (Ex. 6:26), so that in knowledge of the Torah Moses was not greater than Aaron, and Aaron was not greater than Moses.

Happy are these two brothers, who were created only for the glory of Israel.

That is what Samuel said, "It is the Lord that made Moses and Aaron and brought your fathers up" (1 Sam. 12:6).

Thus "Your two breasts are like two fawns:"
this refers to Moses and Aaron.

—Song of Songs Rabbah to Song 4:5

Not only are Moses and Aaron represented through feminine metaphors, so too are Abraham, Isaac, and Jacob, as well as the tribal progenitors, Jacob's sons.

In the following, feminine Israel is ornamented by all of the jewelry contained in the treasure of the Torah: all of the acts of faith are paraded as marks of the beauty of Israel in the explicit setting of Israel's feminine relationship to the masculine God:

Behold, you are beautiful, my love; behold, you are beautiful; your eyes are doves.

"Behold, you are beautiful, my love; behold, you are beautiful; [your eyes are doves]:"

"Behold you are beautiful" in religious deeds,

"Behold you are beautiful" in acts of grace,

"Behold you are beautiful" in carrying out religious obligations of commission,

"Behold you are beautiful" in carrying out religious obligations of omission,

"Behold you are beautiful" in carrying out the religious duties of the home, in separating priestly ration and tithes,

"Behold you are beautiful" in carrying out the religious duties of the field, gleanings, forgotten sheaves, the corner of the field, poor person's tithe, and declaring the field ownerless.

"Behold you are beautiful" in observing the taboo against mixed species.

"Behold you are beautiful" in providing a linen cloak with woolen show-fringes.

"Behold you are beautiful" in [keeping the rules governing] planting,

"Behold you are beautiful" in keeping the taboo on uncircumcised produce,

"Behold you are beautiful" in keeping the laws on produce in the fourth year after the planting of an orchard,

"Behold you are beautiful" in circumcision,

"Behold you are beautiful" in trimming the wound,

"Behold you are beautiful" in reciting the Prayer,

"Behold you are beautiful" in reciting the Shema,

"Behold you are beautiful" in putting a mezuzah on the doorpost of your house,

"Behold you are beautiful" in wearing phylacteries,

"Behold you are beautiful" in building the tabernacle for the Festival of Tabernacles,

"Behold you are beautiful" in taking the palm branch and etrog on the Festival of Tabernacles,

"Behold you are beautiful" in repentance,

"Behold you are beautiful" in good deeds,

"Behold you are beautiful" in this world,

"Behold you are beautiful" in the world to come.

—Song of Songs Rabbah to Song 1:15

Israel, then, is to exhibit the virtues explicitly assigned to women. God responds in a masculine manner. The feminine and masculine virtues complement each other; neither is complete without the other. The process comes to fulfillment in the representation as feminine of all of the virtues, all of the saints and heroes, all of the acts of sanctification that God has commanded and that submissive Israel carries out. Once Israel is feminized, so too is everything else. Then the feminine virtues—submission, trust, perfect loyalty—are adopted by Israel. But that is only for now.

How does the sexual imagery convey deep theological meaning? The message of Song of Songs Rabbah is that, if Israel is feminine now, she will resume her masculinity in the world to come. That is a much more subtle and profound statement, a judgment of the androgyneity of Israel that makes the union of traits, feminine and masculine, something other than a static portrait of a world at rest. In fact, the metaphor of the feminine Israel and the masculine God is subsumed within the more profound message of redemption and carries a critical element in that message: Israel must be patient, submissive, and deeply trusting in God now, so that, in the world to come, Israel may resume its fulfilled masculinity. In this age, Israel to God is as a wife to a husband. But in the age to come, Israel assumes masculine identity. It follows that Israel is represented as androgyne, feminine, then masculine:

R. Berekhiah in the name of R. Samuel b. R. Nahman said, "The Israelites are compared to a woman.

"Just as an unmarried woman receives a tenth part of the property of her father and takes her leave [for her husband's house when she gets married], so the Israelites inherited the land of the seven peoples, who form a tenth part of the seventy nations of the world.

"And because the Israelites inherited in the status of a woman, they said a song in the feminine form of that word, as in the following: 'Then sang Moses and the children of Israel this song [given in the feminine form] unto the Lord' (Ex. 15:1).

"But in the age to come they are destined to inherit like a man, who inherits all of the property of his father.

"That is in line with this verse of Scripture: 'From the east side to the west side: Judah, one portion . . . Dan one, Asher one . . . ' (Ez. 48:7), and so throughout.

"Then they will say a song in the masculine form of that word, as in the following: 'Sing to the Lord a new song' (Ps. 96:1).

"The word 'song' is given not in its feminine form but in its masculine form."

R. Berekiah and R. Joshua b. Levi: "Why are the Israelites compared to a woman?

"Just as a woman takes up a burden and puts it down [that is, becomes pregnant and gives birth], takes up a burden and puts it down, then takes up a burden and puts it down and then takes up no further burden,

"so the Israelites are subjugated and then redeemed, subjugated and then redeemed, but in the end are redeemed and will never again be subjugated.

"In this world, since their anguish is like the anguish of a woman in childbirth, they say the song before him using the feminine form of the word for song,

"but in the age to come, because their anguish will no longer be the anguish of a woman in childbirth, they will say their song using the masculine form of the word for song:

"'In that day this song [in the masculine form of the word] will be sung' (Is. 26:1)."

—Song of Songs Rabbah to Song 5:3

So the real message lies in the femininity of Israel in this world in contrast to its masculinity in the world to come. Not only so, but there is another qualification of considerable urgency.

Feminine Israel is masculine in its aggressive relationship to the nations, and here, once more, we find what we may call temporal—or serial—androgyneity: feminine now, masculine in the age to come. It hardly needs repetition that the system is the work of men and states a masculine viewpoint, which makes the systemic androgyneity all the more remarkable. Israel is one thing to God, another to the nations; feminine and submissive to God, masculine and aggressive to the nations of the world. That point is now fundamental in our characterization of the whole. Israel is feminized only for a time; Israel is fully masculine in the end of time.

Israel is serially androgynous: now feminine, later on, masculine. The following makes this point in respect to God as well, who responds to Israel's character:

> What is your beloved more than another beloved, O fairest among women! What is your beloved more than another beloved, that you thus adjure us?
>
> 5:10 My beloved is all radiant and ruddy, distinguished among ten thousand.
>
> The Israelites answer them, "My beloved is all radiant and ruddy."
>
> "radiant:" to me in the land of Egypt,
>
> "and ruddy:" to the Egyptians.
>
> "radiant:" in the land of Egypt, "For I will go through the land of Egypt" (Ex. 12:13).
>
> "and ruddy:" "And the Lord overthrew the Egyptians" (Ex. 14:27).
>
> "radiant:" at the Sea: "The children of Israel walked upon dry land in the midst of the sea" (Ex. 14:29).
>
> "and ruddy:" to the Egyptians at the Sea: "And the Lord overthrew the Egyptians in the midst of the sea" (Ex. 14:27).
>
> "radiant:" in the world to come.
>
> "and ruddy:" in this world.

R. Levi b. R. Hayyata made three statements concerning the matter:

"'radiant:' on the Sabbath.

"'and ruddy:' on the other days of the week.

"radiant:" on the New Year.

"and ruddy:" on the other days of the year.

"'radiant:' in this world.

"'and ruddy:' in the world to come.

"distinguished among ten thousand:"

Said R. Abba b. R. Kahana, "A mortal king is known by his ceremonial garments, but here, he is fire and his ministers are fire: 'And he came from the myriads holy'" (Dt. 33:2).

"He is marked in the midst of 'the myriads holy.'"

—Song of Songs Rabbah to Song 5:10

Israel now is governed by others, and so is deemed passive, therefore, by the patriarchal document, classified as feminine Israel is whole with God, but God and Israel cannot make peace with the nations of the world except on God's terms. The invocation of the dance, with God as the leader, Israel as the partner, at the end underscores the wholly feminine representation of Israel once more: "like women—like the dance of the righteous." Then feminine Israel plays the role of the wife who stands as mediator between her husband and the world at large; the mother who holds the family together, now the family of the nations and the master, who is God.

As a matter of fact, the emotions encouraged by Judaism in its formative age, such as humility, forbearance, accommodation, a spirit of conciliation, exactly correspond to the political and social requirements of the Jews' condition in that time. And the reason that the same repertoire of emotions persisted with no material change through the unfolding of the writings of the sages of that formative age was the constancy of the Jews' political and social condition. Emotions lay down judgments.

They derive from rational cognition. What Judaism teaches the private person to feel links her or his heart to what Judaism states about the condition of Israel in history and of God in the cosmos. All form one reality, in supernatural world and nature, in time and in eternity wholly consubstantial (so to speak). In the innermost chambers of deepest feelings, the Israelite therefore lives out the public history and destiny of the people, Israel. The genius of Judaism, the reason for its resilience and endurance, lies in its power to teach Jews in private to feel what in public they also must think about the condition of both self and nation. The world within, the world without, are so bonded that one is never alone. The individual's life always is lived with the people. And, we now realize, the virtuous man, as much as the virtuous woman, will exhibit women's virtues of attitude and emotion.

An epitome of the oral Torah's sages' treatment of emotions yields a simple result. Early, middle, and late, a single doctrine and program dictated what people had to say on how Israel should tame its heart. Israel's virtues were to be those of the woman Israel of Song of Songs Rabbah. And it is not difficult to see why. In this world, Israel was a vanquished nation, possessed of a broken spirit. Sages' Judaism for a defeated people prepared the nation for a long future. The vanquished people, the broken-hearted nation that had lost its city and its temple, had, moreover, produced another nation from its midst to take over its scripture and much else. That defeated people, in its intellectuals, as represented in the Rabbinic sources, found refuge in a mode of thought that trained vision to see other things otherwise than as the eyes perceived them. And that general way of seeing things accounts also for the specific matter of the feminization of Israel: Israel now was to endure as a woman, so that, in the age to come, it would resume its masculine position among the nations: dominant and determinative. Among the diverse ways by which the weak and subordinated accommodate to their circumstance, the one of iron-willed pretense in life is most likely to yield the mode of thought at hand: things never are, because they cannot be, what they seem. The uniform tradition on emotions persisted intact because the social realities of Israel's life proved permanent, until, in our own time, they changed. The upshot was that Rabbinic Judaism's Israel was instructed on how to tame its heart and govern its wild emotions, to accept with resignation, to endure with patience, above all, to value the attitudes and emotions that made acceptance and reconciliation into matters of honor and dignity, and, therefore, also made endurance plausible: imitate the feminine virtues.

## DEVIATIONS FROM THE IDEAL

How does the system treat deviation? In narrow terms, we refer to matters that, in Judaism in its classical statement, does not contemplate. Reading the story of the creation of man and woman to state the norm, not only the normal, sages insisted that celibacy and monasticism contradict the way God formed nature: "It is not good for man to be alone; I will make a fitting helper for him" (Gen. 2:18); "Hence a man leaves his father and mother and clings to his wife, so that they become one flesh" (Gen. 2:24). These statements are taken explicitly to require marriage and the making of a family. The law of Judaism, set forth in the Mishnah and amplified in the two Talmuds, does not contemplate spinsterhood. The natural condition of woman, as we shall see in the third part of this chapter, is marriage, and the correct location, a household—an extended family that also formed a unit of economic production. If a woman was widowed or divorced without children, she returned to her father's household until she remarried. It was generally assumed that she would remarry within a year. Childlessness was never by intent. A single model prevailed: the woman married and in charge of her household—exactly as Proverbs, cited at the head of this chapter, indicates.

And yet, were we to complete our account with the preceding paragraph, we should miss the critical, indeed the central, concept of the classical statement of Judaism, one that feminizes the system at its very heart. It is the point at which the system does address deviancy in two of its critical aspects; first, the deviancy represented by ignorance of the Torah, and, second, the deviancy represented by sexuality in the form of prostitution. Here we come across what the Judaic system abhors: failure to master the Torah and therefore to know God as God is self-manifest; and, second, failure to take a position within the social order of holy Israel, God's community. The unlettered man, the society of whores—these represent the outer limits of the Israelite world. And here, we shall now see, we come to the systemic center: the reversal of all rules, the transformation of all values. How so? The ignorant man embodies the highest virtue. The woman ready to sell her body realizes the deepest ideal. And, not only so, but, when all is said and done, it is the virtue represented by the deviant that is set forth as the center and soul of Judaism.

People suppose that the Torah forms the symbolic center of Rabbinic Judaism, and study of the Torah the critical action, so that women, excluded from academies, find no place in Rabbinic Judaism at all; in fact, when we reach the systemic center, we find that "the study of Torah" does not outweigh all else, not at all. Even the stories contained in the Talmud of the land of Israel in which the priority and sanctity of the sage's knowledge of the Torah form the focus of discourse treat study of the Torah as contingent and merely instrumental. Time and again, knowledge of the Torah forms a way station on a path to a more distant, more central goal: attaining *zekhut,* here translated as "the heritage of virtue and its consequent entitlements."

Zekhut embodies the sages' own definition of feminine virtue. Torah study is one means of attaining access to that heritage, of gaining zekhut. There are other equally suitable means, but the merit gained by Torah study is no different from the merit gained by any and all other types of acts of supererogatory grace. Still more astonishing, a single remarkable action may produce zekhut of the same order as a lifetime of devotion to Torah study. A simple ass driver, through a noteworthy act of selfless behavior, may attain the same level of zekhut as a learned sage.

Zekhut is gained for a person by an act of renunciation and self-abnegation, such that Heaven responds with an act of grace. Works of supererogation, which Heaven cannot compel but highly prizes, zekhut defines the very opposite of coercion. It is an act that no one could anticipate or demand, but an act of such remarkable selflessness that Heaven finds itself constrained to respond. That is why the systemic center is formed by an act, on Heaven's part, of responsive grace, meaning grace that one by definition cannot demand or compel, only provoke. When we make ourselves less, Heaven makes us more; but we cannot force our will upon Heaven. When we ask about the feminization of Judaism, our attention rests upon this fact: the right relationship between Israel and God is the relationship that is not coerced, not manipulated, not one defined by a dominant party upon a subordinated one. It is a relationship of mutuality, negotiation, response to what is freely given through what cannot be demanded but only volunteered. The relationship, in other words, is a feminine, not a masculine, one when measured by the prevailing, conventional stereotypes.

It is where Heaven cannot force its will upon us that zekhut intervenes. It is that exquisite balance between our will and Heaven's will that, in the end, brings to its perfect balance and entire fulfillment the exploration of the conflict of God's will and our will that began with Adam and Eve at their last hour in

Eden, and our first hour on earth. And, in context, the fact that we may inherit a treasury of zekhut from our ancestors logically follows: just as we inherit the human condition of the freedom to practice rebellion against God's Word, so we inherit, from former generations, the results of another dimension of the human condition: our power to give willingly what none, even God, can by right or rule compel.

That is why the structure of Israel's political economy rested upon divine response to acts of will consisting of submission, on one's own, to the will of Heaven; these acts endowed Israel with a lien and entitlement upon Heaven. What we cannot by our own will impose, we can by the act of renunciation of our own will evoke. What we cannot accomplish through coercion, we can achieve through submission. God will do for us what we cannot do for ourselves, when we do for God what God cannot make us do. And that means, in a wholly concrete and tangible sense, love God with all the heart, the soul, the might we have. God then stands above the rules of the created world, because God will respond not to what we do in conformity to the rules alone, but also to what we do beyond the requirement of the rules. God is above the rules, and we can gain a response from God when, on some one unique occasion, we too do more than obey—but love spontaneously and all at once, with the whole of our being. That is the conception of God that zekhut, as a conception of power in Heaven and power in humanity, contains. In the relationship between God and humanity expressed in the conception of zekhut, we reach the understanding of what the Torah means when it tells us that we are in God's image and after God's likeness: we are, then, "in our image," the very mirror image of God. God's will forms the mirror image of ours: when we are humble, God responds; when we demand, God withdraws.

When we come to the way in which zekhut is set forth, we find ourselves in a set of narratives of a rather special order.

What is special about them is that women play a critical role, appear as heroines, win the attention and respect of the reader or listener. It is difficult to locate in rabbinic literature before the Talmud of the land of Israel—the Mishnah, the Tosefta, Sifra, for instance—stories in which women figure at all. So to take up a whole series of stories in which women are key players comes as a surprise. But there is more. The storyteller on the surface makes the man the hero; he is the center of the narrative. And yet a second glance at what is coming shows us that the woman precipitates the tale, and her action, not the man's, represents the gift that cannot be compelled but only given; she is the one who freely sacrifices, and she also is represented as the source of wisdom. So our systemic reversal—something above the Torah and the study of the Torah takes priority—is matched by a still less predictable shift in narrative quality, with women portrayed as principal actors.

In all three instances that follow and define what the individual must do to gain zekhut, the point is that the deeds of the heroes of the story make them worthy of having their prayers answered, which is a mark of the working of zekhut. It is supererogatory, uncoerced deeds, those well beyond the strict requirements of the Torah, and even the limits of the law altogether, that transform the hero into a holy man, whose holiness served just like that of a sage marked as such by knowledge of the Torah The story that conveys the concept tells about the zekhut attained by a humble, poor, ignorant man. It is narrated to underline what he has done. But what provokes the event is an act of self-abnegation far greater than that willingly performed by the male hero, which is the woman's readiness to sell herself into prostitution to save her husband. That is not a focus of the story but the given. But nothing has compelled the woman to surrender her body to save her husband; to the contrary, the marital obligations of a woman concern only conventional deeds, which indeed the Mishnah's law maintains may be coerced; failure to do these deeds may result in financial penalties inflicted on the woman in the settlement of her marriage contract. So the story of the uncoerced act of selflessness is told about a man, but occasioned by a woman, and both actors in the story exhibit one and the same virtue.

When Torah stories are told, by contrast, the point is that a man attains zekhut by study of the Torah and a woman attains zekhut by sending her sons and her husband off to study the Torah and sitting home alone—not exactly commensurate action. Only zekhut stories represent the act of the woman as the counterpart and equivalent to the act of the man; and, in fact, even here the fact that the woman's uncoerced gift is far greater than the man's—her body, merely his ass—should not go unnoticed. Once more, we find ourselves at the systemic center, where everything is reversed:

> A certain ass driver appeared before the rabbis [the context requires: in a dream] and prayed, and rain came. The rabbis sent and brought him and said to him, "What is your trade?"
> 
> He said to them, "I am an ass driver."
> 
> They said to him, "And how do you conduct your business?"
> 
> He said to them, "One time I rented my ass to a certain woman, and she was weeping on the way, and I said to her, 'What's with you?' and she said to me, 'The husband of that woman [me] is in prison [for debt], and I wanted to see what I can do to free him.' So I sold my ass and I gave her the proceeds, and I said to her, 'Here is your money, free your husband, but do not sin [by becoming a prostitute to raise the necessary funds].'"
> 
> They said to him, "You are worthy of praying and having your prayers answered."
> 
> —Yerushalmi Taanit 1:4

The ass-driver clearly has a powerful lien on Heaven, so that his prayers are answered, even while those of others are not. What did he do to get that entitlement? He did what no law could demand: impoverished himself to save the woman from a "fate worse than death."

> In a dream of R. Abbahu, Mr. Pentakaka ["Five sins"] appeared, who prayed that rain would come, and it rained. R. Abbahu sent and summoned him. He said to him, "What is your trade?"
>
> He said to him, "Five sins does that man [I] do every day, [for I am a pimp:] hiring whores, cleaning up the theater, bringing home their garments for washing, dancing, and performing before them."
>
> He said to him, "And what sort of decent thing have you ever done?"
>
> He said to him, "One day that man [I] was cleaning the theater, and a woman came and stood behind a pillar and cried. I said to her, 'What's with you?' And she said to me, 'That woman's [my] husband is in prison, and I wanted to see what I can do to free him,' so I sold my bed and cover, and I gave the proceeds to her. I said to her, 'Here is your money, free your husband, but do not sin.'"
>
> He said to him, "You are worthy of praying and having your prayers answered."
>
> —Yerushalmi Taanit 1:4

The named man has done everything sinful that one can do, and, more to the point, he does it every day. So the singularity of the act of zekhut, which suffices if done only one time, encompasses its power to outweigh a life of sin—again, an act of zekhut as the mirror image and opposite of sin. Here again, the single act of saving a woman from a "fate worse than death" has sufficed.

> A pious man from Kefar Imi appeared [in a dream] to the rabbis. He prayed for rain and it rained. The rabbis went up to him. His

householders told them that he was sitting on a hill. They went out to him, saying to him, "Greetings," but he did not answer them.

He was sitting and eating, and he did not say to them, "You break bread too."

When he went back home, he made a bundle of faggots and put his cloak on top of the bundle [instead of on his shoulder].

When he came home, he said to his household [wife], "These rabbis are here [because] they want me to pray for rain. If I pray and it rains, it is a disgrace for them, and if not, it is a profanation of the Name of Heaven. But come, you and I will go up [to the roof] and pray. If it rains, we shall tell them, 'We are not worthy to pray and have our prayers answered.'"

They went up and prayed and it rained.

They came down to them [and asked], "Why have the rabbis troubled themselves to come here today?"

They said to him, "We wanted you to pray so that it would rain."

He said to them, "Now do you really need my prayers? Heaven already has done its miracle."

They said to him, "Why, when you were on the hill, did we say hello to you, and you did not reply?"

He said to them, "I was then doing my job. Should I then interrupt my concentration [on my work]?"

They said to him, "And why, when you sat down to eat, did you not say to us 'You break bread too'?"

He said to them, "Because I had only my small ration of bread. Why would I have invited you to eat by way of mere flattery [when I knew I could not give you anything at all]?"

They said to him, "And why when you came to go down, did you put your cloak on top of the bundle?"

He said to them, "Because the cloak was not mine. It was borrowed for use at prayer. I did not want to tear it."

They said to him, "And why, when you were on the hill, did

your wife wear dirty clothes, but when you came down from the mountain, did she put on clean clothes?"

He said to them, "When I was on the hill, she put on dirty clothes, so that no one would gaze at her. But when I came home from the hill, she put on clean clothes, so that I would not gaze on any other woman."

They said to him, "It is well that you pray and have your prayers answered."

—Yerushalmi Taanit 1:4

Here the woman is at least an equal player; her actions as much as her husband's prove exemplary and illustrate the ultimate wisdom. The pious man finally enjoys the recognition of the sages by reason of his lien upon Heaven, able as he is to pray and bring rain. What has so endowed him with zekhut? Acts of punctiliousness of a moral order: concentrating on his work, avoiding an act of dissimulation, integrity in the disposition of a borrowed object, his wife's concern not to attract other men and her equal concern to make herself attractive to her husband.

We note that, at the systemic center, women find entire equality with men; with no role whatever in the study of the Torah and no possibility of attaining political sagacity, women find a critical place in the sequence of actions that elicit from Heaven the admiring response that zekhut embodies. Indeed, a second reading of the stories shows that the hero is second to the heroine; it is the woman who, in each case, precipitates the occasion for the man's attainment of zekhut, and she, not he, exemplifies the highest pinnacle of selfless virtue. It follows, once more, that those reversals that signal the systemic center culminate in the (for so male a system as this one) ultimate reversal: woman at the height. Just as Torah learning is subordinated, so man is subordinated; zekhut, the gift that can be given but not compelled, like love, in an unerring sense must be called the female virtue that sits atop a male system and structure.

It goes without saying that none of these stories refers explicitly to zekhut; all of them tell us about what it means to enjoy not an entitlement by inheritance alone, but a lien accomplished by one's own supererogatory acts of restraint. Zekhut integrates what has been differentiated. Holding together learning, virtue, and supernatural standing by explaining how Torah study transforms the learning man, zekhut further makes implausible those points of distinction between economics and politics that bore the systemic message of the initial philosophy. Hierarchical classification, with its demonstration of the upward-reaching unity of all being, gives way to a different and more compelling proposition: the unity of all being within the heritage of zekhut, to be attained equally and without differentiation in all the principal parts of the social order. The definition of zekhut therefore carries us to the heart of the integrating and integrated religious system of Judaism. And, we now see, at the center of matters is the virtue that sages themselves classify as feminine and can set forth only in the persons of women.

## WOMEN AND PUBLIC LIFE

From the theology of women in Judaism we turn to the law (Hebrew: *halakhah*) that embodies theology in concrete rules of everyday behavior. Women form a principal, indeed, a generative category for the halakhah, beginning with the Mishnah. The Mishnah is divided into six large topical units, and one of the six is Women, inclusive of family rules. It follows that there, in the details of the laws themselves, we follow the legal system's basic and governing attitude toward women in general. Our interest is not in listing all relevant entries in which women figure, but in characterizing the legal system's very definition of what is at stake when the subject of women comes to the fore.

That formulation of matters permits us to speak of not merely discrete rules concerning women, but the very definition of what we mean when we speak of the feminine. It follows that at stake is not a checklist of discrete rulings but a systematic account of the very definition and position of women in general, the theory that individual rulings express in concrete ways.

In the halakhah as set forth by the Mishnah, women matter in systemic context when, and only when, they relate to men, and men are assumed to form the structure and guarantee the stability of the entire society. In the Mishnah's division of Women, five of the seven tractates of this division are devoted to the formation and dissolution of the marital bond. Of them, three treat what is done by man here on earth—that is, formation of a marital bond through betrothal and marriage contract and dissolution through divorce and its consequences: Qiddushin (betrothals), Ketubot (marriage contracts and their property transfers), and Gittin (writs of divorce). One of them is devoted to what by woman is done here on earth: Sotah (a wife suspected of adultery performs a rite of drinking bitter water; see Num. 5). And Yebamot (Levirate marriages in accord with Deut. 25:10–15), greatest of the seven in size and in formal and substantive brilliance, deals with the corresponding heavenly intervention into the formation and end of a marriage: the effect of death upon the marital bond and the dissolution, through death, of that bond. The other two tractates, Nedarim (vows) and Nazir (the vow of the Nazirite; see Num. 6), draw into one the two realms of reality, Heaven and earth, as they work out the effects of vows taken by women and subject to the confirmation or abrogation of the father or husband. These vows make a deep impact on the marital life of the woman who has taken such a vow. So, in all, the division and its system delineate the natural and supernatural character of the woman's role in the social economy framed by man: the beginning, end, and middle of that relationship.

The Mishnaic system of women thus focuses on the two crucial stages in the transfer of women and of property from one domain to another: (1) the leaving of the father's house to the husband through marriage, and (2) the leaving of the husband's house at the marriage's dissolution through divorce or through the husband's death or the wife's infidelity. There is yet a third point of interest, though it is much less important than these first two stages: the duration of the marriage. But the handful of rules on that subject hardly matches the enormous and dense corpus of laws on betrothal, marriage contracts, divorce, levirate marriage and the dissolution thereof, and the wife accused of adultery, with fundamental consequences for the continuation or the dissolution of the marriage. Finally, included within the division and at a few points relevant to women in particular are rules of vows in general and of the special vow to be a Nazir; the former included because, in the scriptural treatment of the theme, the rights of the father or husband to annul the vows of a daughter or wife form the central problematic, and the latter included for no very clear reason except that it is a species of which the vow is the genus.

To the message and the purpose of the Mishnaic system of women, woman is essential and central. But she is not critical. She sets the stage for the processes of the sacred. It is she who can be made sacred to man. It is she who ceases to stand within a man's sacred circle. But God, through supernature, and man, through the documentary expression of his will and intention, possess the active power of sanctification. Women for the division of Women define a principal component of the Mishnah's orderly conception of reality. Women form a chief component of the six-part realm of the sacred. It is, as I said, their position in the social economy of the Israelite reality, natural and supernatural, which is the subject of the division and its tractates. But the whole is always important in *relationship* to man on earth and God in Heaven.

The Mishnah is produced within and can only imagine a patriarchal society. Its legislation on women to begin with expresses the values of that society. This is self-evident in that the critical points of the system—beginning, end of marriage—define what is important about woman. What requires close attention and regulation is important because the relationship of woman to man constitutes the criterion of significance. Women's relationships to other women never come under discussion, except as a realm from which a woman may not be wholly cut off at her husband's whim. But if there were activities used by women as a basis for female solidarity and worth, the Mishnah does not legislate about them.

Since it is what the Mishnah deems important that the Mishnah chooses for its careful scrutiny, the point is obvious. The Mishnah does not imagine that men live apart from women or that women exist outside of relationship with, and therefore control of, men. The Mishnah is a man's document and imagines a man's world. Women have rights, protected by man and Heaven alike. But these rights pertain, specifically, to the relationship of women to men (and Heaven), and specified among them is none of consequence outside of male society. The reason is that relationship is derivative and dependent upon that to which relationship is formed. Man is at the center. That fact makes all the more striking the contrary perspective set forth in other documents in the canon of the Judaism of the dual Torah, also produced by men, also expressive of a male viewpoint—by definition: woman as the model of inner virtue, woman as the point of systemic reversal.

The Mishnah's system addresses and means to create an ordered and well-regulated world. The Mishnah states that which is the order and regulation for such a world. That explains the point at which women become important in the legal part of the Judaic system: when women move from one setting and status to another. What defines the woman's status—what is rarely made explicit in the division of Women—is not whether or not she may have sexual relations, but with whom she may have them and with what consequence. It is assumed that, from long before the advent of puberty, a girl may be married and in any event is a candidate for sexuality. From puberty onward she will be married. But what is selected for intense and continuing concern is with whom she may legitimately do so, and with what economic and social effect. There is no sexual deed without public consequence; and only rarely will a sexual deed not yield economic results, in the aspect of the transfer of property from one hand to another. So what is anomalous is the woman's sexuality, which is treated in a way wholly different from man's. And the goal and purpose of Mishnah's division of Women are to bring under control and force into stasis all of the wild and unruly potentialities of sexuality, with their dreadful threat of uncontrolled shifts in personal status and material possession alike.

The Mishnah invokes Heaven's interest in this most critical moment for individual and society alike. Its conception is that what is rightly done on earth is confirmed in Heaven. A married woman who has sexual relations with any man but her husband has not merely committed a crime on earth, she has sinned against Heaven. It follows that when a married woman receives a writ of divorce and so is free to enter into relationships with any man of her choosing, the perceptions of that woman are affected in Heaven just as much as are those of man on earth. What was beforehand a crime and a sin afterward is holy, not subject to punishment at all. The woman may contract a new marriage on earth which Heaven, for its part, will oversee and sanctify. What is stated in these simple propositions is that those crucial and critical turnings at which a woman changes hands produce concern and response in Heaven above as much as on earth below. Heaven is invoked specifically at those times and in those circumstances in which the Mishnah confronts a situation of anomaly or disorder and proposes to effect suitable regulation and besought order. What Judaism says about women it says about every other critical topic in its system. And the message, whether in the form of theology or of law, remains the same.

CHAPTER 4

# *Hinduism*

Traditional Hinduism, like the other world religions, displays a deep ambivalence about the nature and proper role of women. In the sacred texts of this religion—texts composed almost exclusively by men—women have been portrayed as the pillars of society and the family, but also as intrinsically weak and untrustworthy; as objects of reverence and worship and as inherently driven by lust and desire; as dependent on and devoted to men but also naturally inclined to aggressiveness and dangerous lack of constraint.

Such ambivalence pervades the major social roles assigned to women in patriarchal Hinduism (that is, mother and wife) and is also projected into the theological arena. Hindu goddesses, in all the periods of this religion's long history, have reflected the ambiguity surrounding Hindu women. Goddesses, like their human counterparts, are often simultaneously worshiped and feared; they can be benevolent and maternal but also malevolent and threatening—the source of both life and death. Some Hindu goddesses, such as Sita, are the apotheosis of the submissive and devoted wife, whereas others (for example, the warriorlike Durga or the fearsome and bloodthirsty Kali) represent the active and dominating form of "woman." Goddesses of the latter sort, often referred to as "Mother" and worshiped as the principal deity by both men and women, are not easily assimilated into a stereotypical portrait of traditional, patriarchal religion.

While such conflicting visions of the female, human and divine, point to deep-seated psychological hopes and fears on the part of males, they have also been institutionalized and, to some extent at least, interiorized by many Hindu women. But even as some of these attitudes and prejudices have served to limit the roles of women in Hindu society (past and present), others have provided scope for social acceptance of alternatives to unmitigated patriarchal subjugation. For if, on the one hand, Hindu ideology represents the ideal woman as submissive wife, nurturing mother, and the model of subservient religious devotion and service, it also allows for an ideal of a different sort: woman as the embodiment of *sakti*, or cosmic energy and power.

It is somewhat difficult, therefore, to speak of "deviations" from a single "ideal" of female virtue in this religion. Rather, Hinduism provides a set of different kinds of religious, moral, and social ideals for women—each with its own set of possibilities and ambivalences. From the ancient past to the present day, Hinduism has presented a variety of religious models for women and a range of different visions of the divine female; it has both severely restricted or even prohibited women from leadership roles in public and religious life, but has also accepted the participation of women who have assumed those roles. With these ambivalences and range of possibilities in mind, let us turn to an examination of the various kinds of models Hinduism has put forward for the "ideal woman" and the positions women have assumed in the various traditions that make up Hinduism.

## MODELS OF VIRTUE FOR WOMEN THROUGH THE LIFE CYCLE

In the Hindu law book known as the *Laws of Manu* (Manu-smrti), composed around the turn of the Common Era, one type of ideal for women is laid out in the following passage:

A girl, a young woman, or even an old woman should not do anything independently, even in (her own) house. In childhood a woman should be under her father's control, in youth under her husband's, and when her husband is dead, under her sons'. She should not have independence. A woman should not try to separate herself from her father, her husband, or her sons, for her separation from them would make both (her own and her husband's) families contemptible. She should always be cheerful, and clever at household affairs; she should keep her utensils well polished and not have too free a hand in spending. When her father, or her brother with her father's permission, gives her to someone, she should obey that man while he is alive and not violate her vow to him when he is dead.

—Manusmrti 5.147–51[1]

Here we have a classic formulation of male dominance: a woman should be under a man's control and guidance at every stage of life. A girl's father should supervise her in her childhood, her husband in her youth and middle age, and if she survives her husband she should be placed under the care of her sons—such is the way to prevent families from becoming "contemptible." The ideal woman here and elsewhere is not only submissive to her male family members but is wholly occupied with the pursuits of domesticity. She should carefully but "cleverly" run the household affairs (under the supervision of a male) and keep herself focused on her chores. Marriage is for life, without the possibility of divorce for the woman, and remarriage, should the husband die first, is strictly forbidden.

The virtuous woman who conforms to this model is equated with "the goddesses of good fortune," worthy of worship by her menfolk. She is the linchpin for the proper performance of a householder's dharma, or religious duty, which includes the procreation and care of children, the running of the household, and sexual pleasure (or kama, one of the prescribed "ends of life" for the Hindu in the householder stage of life), but also the attainment of heaven itself for the male householder and his ancestors:

> There is no difference at all between the goddesses of good fortune who live in houses and women who are the lamps of their houses, worthy of reverence and greatly blessed because of their progeny. The wife is the visible form of what holds together the begetting of children, the caring for them when they are born, and the ordinary business of every day. Children, the fulfillment of duties, obedience, and the ultimate sexual pleasure depend upon a wife, and so does heaven, for oneself and one's ancestors. The woman who is not unfaithful to her husband but restrains her mind-and-heart, speech, and body reaches her husband's worlds (after death), and good people call her a virtuous woman.
> —Manusmrti 9.2629

The "virtuous woman," defined here in terms of her faithfulness to her husband and her yogiclike restraint of her mind, speech, and bodily desires, is crucial to the success of the family. In this same text, it is said that women who fulfill such an ideal should be "revered," for through their virtue and the respect paid to them by their male family members the gods are pleased and the family thrives. Conversely, in homes where virtuous women are not so honored and become unhappy, the family is destroyed:

> Fathers, brothers, husbands, and brothers-in-law who wish for great good fortune should revere these women and adorn them. The deities delight in places where women are revered, but where women are not revered all rites are fruitless. Where the women of the family are miserable, the family is soon destroyed, but it always thrives where the women are not miserable. Homes that are cursed by women of the family who have not been treated with

due reverence are completely destroyed, as if struck down by witchcraft. Therefore men who wish to prosper should always revere these women with ornaments, clothes, and food at celebrations and festivals. There is unwavering good fortune in a family where the husband is always satisfied by the wife, and the wife by the husband. . . . Through bad marriages, the neglect of rites, failure to study the Veda, and transgressing against priests, families cease to be families.

—Manusmrti 3.55–60, 63

Here, then, is one standard for the Hindu woman: wholly dependent on her male family members, she is assigned her place in the home where she is charged with the production and proper upbringing of children and the supervision of domestic affairs. She is to remain restrained in mind and body and absolutely faithful to her husband, and if she does so the husband is to regard her as a kind of goddess. Her role is pivotal to wellbeing of both the family as a whole and to the fate of her husband, and she in turn should be accorded the respect and good treatment she deserves.

Such a portrait of the exemplary woman and her important role in the life of her husband and family found theological and mythological expression in the figures of several Hindu goddesses. Many of the goddesses of the Hindu pantheon are portrayed as wives or consorts of certain Hindu gods—Parvati connected to Siva, Radha to Krishna, Sri to Vishnu—and provide divine models and embodiments of the virtues of the devoted wife as outlined in the law books. Moreover, these goddesses serve as both mediators between the great male gods and human beings and as exemplary devotees, paragons of religious devotion for both male and female humans.

The epitome of the ideal Hindu wife—utterly devoted and loyal to her husband—is found in the figure of the goddess Sita, wife of god-king Rama. At one point in the narrative of the great epic called the Ramayana, Rama is banished from his kingdom and exiled to the wilderness. Rama proposes to leave Sita in the city because he thinks she could not bear the discomforts of the forest. Sita insists on following her husband, threatening even to kill herself if forced to separate from him; the husband's fate is that of the wife, and devotion to him is the "single goal for a woman":

> A wife wins the fate of her husband, and not her own, O bull of a man. Knowing this, I shall live in the forest from now on. Here and hereafter there is only a single goal for a woman: her lord, and not her father, her child, herself, her mother nor her friends. . . . O take me with you, noble husband! Do as I ask, for my heart is devoted only to you. If you leave without me, I shall die![2]

Later in the story, Sita is abducted by the wicked Ravana and taken to the island of Lanka, where she is held hostage. Throughout her abduction, however, Sita remains unswervingly loyal to Rama—and to her religious duty:

> I cannot be seduced by wealth or glory. I belong only to Raghava [Rama] as light belongs to the sun. After having leaned on the honored arm of that world-protector, how could I ever turn to anyone else? I am the proper wife of the lord of the earth; I belong to him as the law belongs to a self-aware Brahmin [priest] who has faithfully kept his vows.[3]

But Sita's loyalty to her husband (a kind of metaphor for the human being's devotion to God, even under trying circumstances) is tested to even a greater extent when, after being rescued by Rama, the latter doubts her fidelity during the period of captivity. Distraught by Rama's false accusations, Sita no longer wishes to live and enters the fire of her own funeral pyre. But because of her innocence, the god of fire refuses to harm her; Rama, finally convinced of her purity, takes her back.

On a symbolic level, Sita's faithfulness to Rama even when he apparently abandons her serves as a cautionary tale about the need for devotion to God under the most trying of circumstances—that is, even when God appears to have abandoned the devotee. But the figure of Sita also carries with her more particular and gendered messages concerning one type of ideal for the Hindu woman and wife. "The husband is as a God to the woman," says Sita. "[H]e is her family, and her *guru*. Therefore, even at the price of her life, she must seek to please her lord."[4]

## DEVIATIONS FROM THE IDEAL

This outline of the ideally dependent, submissive, and utterly faithful woman is sketched on a background that assumes a rather different notion of the inherent nature of women. Left to her own devices, some texts assert, women will follow their intrinsic and evil proclivities. By nature, women are said to be lustful and unfaithful, unable to control their sexual desires. Such natural promiscuity is even said to be wholly indiscriminate:

> Good looks do not matter to them, nor do they care about youth; "A man!" they say, and enjoy sex with him, whether he is good-looking or ugly. By running after men like whores, by their fickle minds, and by their natural lack of affection these women are unfaithful to their husbands even when they are zealously guarded here. Knowing that their very own nature is like this, as it was born at the creation by the Lord of Creatures, a man should make the utmost effort to guard them. The bed and the seat, jewelry, lust, anger, crookedness, a malicious nature, and bad conduct are what Manu assigned to women. There is no ritual with Vedic verses for women; this is a firmly established point of law. For women, who have no virile strength and no Vedic verses, are falsehood; this is well established.
>
> —Manusmrti 9.14–18

Such an extremely unflattering view of women as "by nature" promiscuous, untrustworthy, and evil—the very essence of "falsehood"—is replicated in a variety of ancient texts. "There exist no friendships with women," says the most ancient of Hindu texts, the Rg Veda, for "they have the hearts of hyenas" (Rg Veda 10.95.15). Elsewhere in that text we read that women are ineducable (Rg Veda 8.33.17), an early sanction for the prohibition of teaching women the sacred texts of the Veda. The somewhat later Mahabharata declares that "women are speakers of untruth," that "fickleness is the norm in women," that "women are the root of faults and have weak understanding," and that "nothing exists that is more wicked than women" (Mahabharata 1.68.72; 5.36.56; 13.38.1; 13.38.12).

These kinds of assumptions about women justify the insistence that men must guard and protect women from their own inborn proclivities. The following text claims this is in fact the husband's "supreme duty" and suggests the best way to guard one's wife is to keep her busy at home and indoctrinate her so thoroughly that she "guards herself":

> Men must make their women dependent day and night, and keep under their own control those who are attached to sensory objects. Her father guards her in childhood, her husband guards her in youth, and her sons guard her in old age. A woman is not fit for independence. . . . Women should especially be guarded against addictions, even trifling ones, for unguarded (women) would bring sorrow upon both families (her own and her husband's). Regarding this as the supreme duty of all the classes, husbands, even weak ones, try to guard their wives. For by zealously guarding his wife he guards his own descendants, practices, family, and himself, as well as his own duty. . . . No man is able to guard women entirely by force, but they can be entirely guarded by using these means: he should keep her busy amassing and spending money, engaging in purification, attending to her duty, cooking food, and

looking after the furniture. Women are not guarded when they are confined in a house by men who can be trusted to do their jobs well; but women who guard themselves are well guarded. Drinking, associating with bad people, being separated from their husbands, wandering about, sleeping, and living in other peoples' houses are the six things that corrupt women.

—Manusmrti 9.2–3, 5–7, 10–13

But if certain Hindu texts thus represent women as inherently unfaithful and lustful, other texts—especially those that were composed within traditions that emphasize devotion, or *bhakti*, to a loving God—transform the supposed erotic nature of women and depict it as both a spiritual tool and as a trope for the longing and desire of the human for God. In songs, poems, and myths concerning Krishna and his playful dalliances with the cow-herder women known as the *gopis*, sexuality is placed in the service of an emotionalistic attachment to the divine. The gopis, often portrayed as married women, are lured by Krishna from their homes and husbands and they join the deity in ecstatic dance and sexually charged flirtations. Radha, one of the gopis herself, is portrayed as the very incarnation of the longing for the elusive lover—which is no other than the longing for an inscrutable, apparently fickle, and sometimes distant God:

> My heart values his vulgar ways,
> refuses to admit my rage,
> feels strangely elated,
> and keeps denying his guilt.
> When he steals away without me
> to indulge his craving
> for more young women,
> my perverse heart
> only wants Krishna back.
> What can I do?[5]

The evocation of "love in separation," which ratchets up the desire for the lover (that is, God) to its highest levels, is sometimes complemented by the notion that the most powerful desire is that for one "who belongs to another." Illicit love on the part of the woman, in other words, is regarded in certain devotional traditions as a metaphor for a love of God that transcends the strictures of ordinary morality. Radha is in some traditions said to be a married woman who throws away her reputation out of an overwhelming desire for Krishna:

> I who body and soul
> am at your beck and call,
> was a girl of noble family.
> I took no thought for what would be said of me,
> I abandoned everything.[6]

The legend of the sixteenth-century female poet-saint Mirabai claims that, although married to a prince, she refused to consummate the union because of her devotion to Krishna. Despite the disapproval of both society and the royal family (the prince's mother is said to have tried to poison Mirabai), her erotic/spiritual attachment to God is described in heroic terms:

> Mira unraveled the fetters of family;
>   she sundered the chains of shame to sing
>   of her mountain-lifting Lover and Lord.
> Like a latter-day gopi, she showed the meaning
>   of devotion in our devastated age.
> She had no fear. Her impervious tongue
>   intoned the triumphs of her artful Lord.
> Villains thought it vile. They set out to kill her,
>   but not even a hair on her head was harmed,
> For the poison she took turned elixir in her throat.
>   She cringed before none: she beat love's drum.[7]

If, then, women are negatively evaluated as overly sensual and even lascivious in some Hindu law books, in other texts they are depicted as reorienting this "natural" eroticism around the love of and devotion to God. While such devotionalistic texts do not exactly condone the abandonment of the ideal of the faithful and subservient wife and mother, they do provide an alternative model of women whose devotion to the deity takes precedence over all other worldly concerns. Female sensuality and desire, when properly directed toward the divine, are in certain forms of Hinduism encouraged rather than feared and repressed.

Yet another representation of woman is displayed in the mythology surrounding a class of Hindu goddesses whose characteristics drastically diverge from the ideals described above. Figures like the warrior-goddess Durga represent a radically different form of the feminine; neither the subservient wife nor the devoted lover of a male deity, Durga is a powerful and independent goddess whose exploits include the vanquishing of demons and whose personality is hardly meek and subservient. Riding on a lion and depicted with weapons in each of her many hands, Durga is especially well known for her defeat of a demon who had taken the shape of a buffalo:

> When his own army was totally destroyed, the buffalo demon assumed his own buffalo form and terrified the troops of the Goddess. Some he struck with his muzzle; others he trampled with his hooves. Some he lashed with his tail and pierced with his two horns; others he rushed at and roared at and whirled around; and still others he hurled down upon the surface of the earth by means of the hurricane of his breath. When he had thus felled the vanguard of the Goddess's army, the great demon attacked her lion in order to kill him, and then the Mother became angry. . . . When the fierce Goddess saw the great demon attacking, swollen thus with anger, she became frantic to slay him. . . . Enraged by this,

the furious mother of the universe drank the supreme wine again and again; her eyes became red, and she laughed. The demon roared, puffed up and intoxicated with his own strength and courage, and with his two horns he hurled mountains at the furious Goddess, but she pulverized his missiles with a hail of arrows. ... Thus the demon named Buffalo was destroyed by the Goddess, together with his army and her band of friends, when he had bewitched the triple world. And when the buffalo had fallen, all creatures in the triple world, along with all the gods and demons and men, shouted "Victory!"[8]

Durga seems to represent a vision of the female that challenges and inverts that of the traditional Hindu law books. Wholly independent (and not at all in need) of male protection and guidance, Durga is the incarnation of the feminine cosmic power or energy (known as Sita) that invigorates the universe. She is action or power personified, the very embodiment of the creative force. She is, therefore, the "Mother" (and not "the wife," as in the case of Sakti, but she is also clearly a destroyer, a dangerous and almost demented warrior whose deathly fury is virtually uncontrollable.

Such a complex vision of the "Mother" is even more apparent in the figure of Kali, the goddess of cosmic illusion or "magic" *(maya),* of the material nature of reality, and of time. She is said to pervade all aspects of the universe, the Mother of all creation, but her unpredictability and chaotic nature is also hinted at in the following, where she is called the "mad Goddess":

> O Mother! Thou art present in every form;
> Thou art in the entire universe and in its tiniest
>     and most trifling things.
> Wherever I go and wherever I look,
> I see Thee, Mother, present in thy cosmic form,
> The whole world—earth, water, fire, and air—

> All are thy forms, O Mother, the whole world of birth and
>     death. . . . O Mother! Who can understand Thy magic?
> Thou art a mad Goddess; Thou has made all mad with
>     attachment.⁹

Other texts are more explicit about Kali's capriciousness, her "madness," her bloodthirsty nature, and her association with death. Embracing such a goddess as the "Mother" is a means of both accepting and seeking refuge from the darker forces of life and the inevitability of death:

> I am lying at Thy feet, O Mother, Thou dost not
>     look at me even once.
> Thou art engrossed in Thy play, O Kali, Thou art
>     immersed in Thy thought.
> What play dost Thou play on earth, in heaven and hell?
> All close their eyes in terror and cry "Mother!"
>     "Mother!" grasping Thy feet.
> O Mother! Thou has great dissolution in Thy hand;
>     Siva lies at Thy feet, absorbed in bliss.
> Thou laughest aloud (striking terror); streams of
>     blood flow from Thy limbs.
> O Tara, doer of good, the good of all, grantor of safety,
>     O Mother, grant me safety.
> O Mother Kali! take me in Thy arms; O Mother Kali!
> Take me in Thy arms.¹⁰

While a figure like Kali calls out for psychological interpretation—she does, at least in part, represent conflicting and overdetermined attitudes about the mother—both she and Durga have provided the Hindu tradition with a vision of the female that is both starkly in contradiction to other ideals and yet offers sanctions for capabilities among women that invert such traditional ideals. Although Durga and Kali are certainly not role models for Hindu women, they do present theological precedents for the cultural acceptance of a person like Indira Gandhi, the former prime minister of India and one of the most powerful female leaders and stateswomen of the modern world.

## WOMEN AND PUBLIC LIFE

Given these differing images and ideals of women in Hinduism, it is not surprising that the tradition also displays an ambivalence about the possible participation of women in public and religious life. On the one hand, and in keeping with the image of woman as dependent and subservient, women have often been prohibited from independent action outside of the home and their participation in religious rituals is sometimes entirely subsumed within the husband's activity. But on the other hand, women have also assumed important roles in public and religious life in all periods of the history of this religion, and in some cases have become cultural and religious leaders in their own right.

Such ambivalence concerning the role of women is in evidence already in the earliest period of religious history in India. In the Vedic era, religion revolved around the ideology and performance of the fire sacrifice. Offerings of various sorts (cakes made from grain, animals, and the juice of the soma plant) were made to one or another of the many Vedic deities with the expectation that these deities would return to the sacrificer various rewards: good crops, sons, wealth and power in this world, and a place in heaven in the afterlife. In all forms of sacrifice, ranging from the simple rites of the householder to the incredibly intricate rituals of the "public," or *srauta,* cult, the participation of women was both extremely circumscribed and absolutely necessary.

Women were, as a rule, forbidden to act as sacrificers on their own and were generally relegated to a kind of ornamental status within the ritual, and yet their attendance and participation as wives of sacrificers were regarded as essential for the proper performance of the sacrifice. Unless he has taken a wife, a man is excluded from the all-important ritual of sacrifice, for the male sacrificer is said to be "completed" by his wife: "It is known from tradition that half of oneself is the wife" (Baudhayana Srauta Sutra 29.9). Husband and wife together "become yoked like oxen in the sacrifice" (Taittiriya Brahmana 3.7.5.11) and share in its responsibilities and benefits. It is as a pair that husband and wife participate in the sacrificial rituals; they are jointly responsible for both its obligations and the merit that comes from fulfilling the sacrificial duties. The wife is thus said in at least one text to be "qualified to perform sacrifices" because she assumes the responsibilities for carrying out the rituals on her own when her husband cannot:

> Together do these two (husband and wife) constitute a couple; together do these two maintain the sacred fires; together do these two procreate and obtain progeny. The eastern world pertains to the husband, the western world to the wife. Since the wife takes upon herself the responsibility of the vow (to maintain the sacrificial rites) of the husband who has gone out on a journey or who has become incapacitated, therefore she is entitled to half (of the ritual's benefits). Women are (thus) qualified to perform sacrifices.
> —Manava Srauta Sutra 8.23.10–14

Even within the ordinarily limited role women had within the Vedic sacrifice, their very presence infused the ritual with important values and concerns centering around domesticity and the welfare of the home, sexuality and fertility, hospitality, and exchange. Women thus assumed a critical function as mediators in Vedic society and religion. A recent study concludes that the ideal Vedic wife "plays a crucial role in knitting together her community. By producing sons, she ensures the linkage of generations and the continued veneration of the ancestors. By dispensing food and hospitality, she forges harmonious links between different segments of secular Aryan society. By her role in *srauta* ritual (and by making such ritual possible) she links gods and men and allows the religious life of the community to proceed."[11]

In the middle centuries of the first millennium before the Common Era, the rise of world renunciation and asceticism challenged some of the premises of the Vedic sacrificial cult and brought to the fore an emphasis on new religious goals and methods: the search for liberation from rebirth and the cultivation of detachment from sensuality and desire, yogic discipline, and meditation on the true nature of the cosmos and life in it. Beginning in this period and extending through the subsequent history of Hinduism, a strong strain of world renunciation and asceticism colored attitudes toward women. For males who pursued such a life, which included a vow of chastity, women were often depicted as temptresses on the path to desirelessness and detachment. Mythological texts abound in stories of human or semidivine women who cause the downfall of male ascetics.

But the tradition also provides examples of women who themselves are in search for philosophical truth and spiritual liberation. Already in the early Upanishads, texts composed beginning in about the seventh century B.C.E., one reads of women who participate in the theological discussions concerning ultimate reality and truth and are bent upon obtaining liberation (or "immortality"). One such case is Maitreyi, one of the wives of the famous sage and teacher Yajnavalkya:

> Now, Yajnavalkya had two wives, Maitreyi and Katyayani. Of the two, Maitreyi was a woman who took part in theological discussions, while Kityayi's understanding was limited to womanly matters. One day, as he was preparing to undertake a different mode

of life (i.e., preparing to renounce the world), Yajnavalkya said: "Maitreyi. I am about to go away from this place. So come, let me make a settlement between you and Katyayani." Maitreyi asked in reply: "If I were to possess the entire world filled with wealth, sir, would it, or would it not, make me immortal?" "No," said Yajnavalkya, "it will only permit you to live the life of a wealthy person. Through wealth one cannot expect immortality." "What is the point in getting something that will not make me immortal?" retorted Maitreyi. "Tell me instead, sir, all that you know."

—Brhadaranyaka Upanishad 4.5.1–4[12]

Yajnavalkya thereupon discourses to his wife on the true nature of the self *(atman)* "'on which one should reflect and concentrate. For . . . when one has reflected and concentrated on one's self, one knows this whole world. . . . There, I have given you the instruction, Maitreyi. That's all there is to immortality.' After saying this, Yajnavalkya went away." (4.5.6, 15).

Women ascetics, philosophers, and religious teachers, or gurus, though rare, are nevertheless known to the Hindu tradition. In recent years, women have played important roles in several groups that center around a male guru, and certain female gurus have emerged and gained considerable following both in India and in the West.

The vast majority of women in Hinduism (like the vast majority of men) do not renounce the world but rather are guided by the religious strictures governing life within society. In response to the world-renouncing traditions inaugurated in the middle centuries of the first millennium B.C.E., Hindu texts began to emphasize the importance of dharma, or the religious duties associated with one's class or caste and stage of life. Within and between the stages of life are prescribed life-cycle rites, the most important of which are the initiation ceremony (regarded as a "second birth" and inaugurating the first stage of life as a religious student under the guidance of a guru) and marriage (which marks the beginning of the stage of life as a householder). These life-cycle rites are called *samskaras* and are designed to gradually perfect the mind and body of the individual and render one capable of performing other rituals.

The full complement of life-cycle rites were only for males; women were specifically precluded from the study of Veda in the first stage of life and therefore did not undergo the initiation ceremony. Those rites of passage that women did undergo were performed without the ritual accompaniment of recited verses from the Veda, for women were traditionally prohibited from even hearing the sound of this sacred text. Nevertheless, in the following passage certain of the important life-cycle rites, stages of life, and subsequent ritual duties of the male householder are equated to their supposed correlates in the woman's life:

> For women, this cycle (of rites of passage) should be performed without Vedic verses, leaving nothing else out, at the proper time and in the proper order, to perfect the body. The ritual of marriage is traditionally known as the Vedic initiation ritual for women; serving her husband is (the equivalent of) living with a guru, and household chores are the rites of the fire.
>
> —Manusmrti 2.66–67

The domestic life of the dependent woman is here valorized by connecting it to the religious life of men: marriage is equated to the initiation ceremony, service to the husband is correlated to the study of the Veda under the tutelage of a *guru*, and household chores are regarded as the female equivalent of the sacrificial rituals performed by the husband.

The duties, or dharma, of a woman, under this view, revolve entirely around affairs of the home, the family, and the marriage. In a summary of the "duty of the woman" *(stri-dharma),* one author conflates the woman's religious duties with her "service to her husband":

The husband is thus to be propitiated (by the wife as follows): by observing the rules of purification; by attending to the fire ritual; by paying homage to guests; by taking care of the household duties; by keeping close watch over the household (accounts), both income and expenditure; by attending to her husband's bodily comfort; by serving food to her husband's dependents, etc.; . . . by love-making and so on at night; by avoiding both those things which are forbidden to her and those which her husband does not like; by putting into practice both those things which are prescribed and those which her husband likes; . . . by obedient service to her husband; and by doing what he says. Propitiating him in this way is said to constitute true "service" to one's husband.[13]

Among the most controversial elements of this traditional view of a woman's religious duties is the ritual called *sati*. This practice, relatively common especially among the upper classes (and most especially among women from the warrior castes) from the eighth century C.E. onward, entailed the self-sacrifice of the widow who joined her deceased husband on his funereal pyre. Sati, which literally means the "virtuous woman," was regarded by some Hindu women as both the ultimate act of devotion to the husband and as a preferable alternative to life as a widow. The following depicts a queen's conversation with her son, who was trying to prevent her from cremating herself in the fire:

> If at this hour my regard is not towards you, it is that my lord's great condescension comes between us. Furthermore, dear son, I am not ever craving for the sight of another lord. I am the lady of a great house, born of stainless ancestry, one whose virtue is her dower. . . . Daughter, spouse, mother of heroes, how otherwise could such a woman as I, whose price was valour, act? . . . I would die while still unwidowed. I cannot endure, like the widowed Rati, to make unavailing lamentations for a burnt husband. Going before, like the dust of your father's feet, to announce his coming to the heavens, I shall be high esteemed of the hero-loving

spouses of the gods.... Not to die, but to live at such a time would be unfeeling. Compared with the flame of wifely sorrow, whose fuel is imperishable love, fire itself is chilly cold.... Not in the body, dear son, but in the glory of loyal widows would I abide on earth. Therefore dishonour me no more, I beseech you, beloved son, with opposition to my heart's desire.... Having embraced her son and kissed his head, the queen went forth on foot from the women's quarter, and, though the heavens, filled with the citizen's lamentations, seemed to block her path, proceeded to the Sarasvati's banks. Then, having worshiped the fire with the blooming red lotus posies of a woman's timorous glances, she plunged into it, as the moon's form enters the adorable sun.[14]

The practice of sati became a major issue among both the British colonial rulers and Hindu reformers in the beginning of the early nineteenth century and was officially outlawed in 1829. Nevertheless, satis have occurred occasionally since; one recent case in north India received much media attention and was the cause of great controversy.

The rise of the worship of goddesses in various forms in the middle to late part of the first millennium C.E. had as one of its expressions the emergence of highly secretive sects in which acts prohibited by the orthodox were practiced under ritual conditions in order to gain spiritual power and salvation. These traditions, known collectively as Tantricism, assumed a bipolar cosmos, conceived of in gendered terms as the male and female principles. The goal of many such groups was to reunite the male principle (sometimes equated with the god Siva) and the female principle (the goddess or the active energy of the universe called Sakti). This metaphysical union was enacted in ceremonies where the male practitioner constituted himself as Siva and his female consort as the goddess and engaged in ritual sex: "Viewing the Sakti as Gauri (the wife of Siva) and himself as Siva, he should pronounce the root-mantra (i.e., the magical spell) of his chosen deity and should offer the father-face into the mother-face (i.e., he should engage in ritual copulation)."[15] Although women participants in Tantric cults remained largely passive and did not assume positions of leadership, they did play a crucial—even cosmic—role in the ritual practices of such groups.

The popularity of various traditions and movements centering around devotion, or bhakti, to a personalized, loving god provided even greater new opportunities for participation of women in the religious life of Hinduism. As early as the composition of the Bhagavad Gita (ca. 200 B.C.E.–200 C.E.), the restrictive nature of early religious formulations were lifted; devotionalism opened up the possibility of salvation even to those most despised by the higher castes. Women, too, were from this point on given access to the divine; they, like criminals, commoners, and those of the lowest rank in caste Hinduism, could "reach the highest way" if they only devoted themselves solely to God. Krishna, the principal deity of the Bhagavad Gita, tells disciple Arjuna that

> If he is devoted solely to me, even a violent criminal must be deemed a man of virtue, for his resolve is right. His spirit quickens to sacred duty, and he finds eternal peace; Arjuna, know that no one devoted to me is lost. If they rely on me, Arjuna, women, commoners, men of low rank, even men born in the womb of evil, reach the highest way. . . . Keep me in your mind and devotion, sacrifice to me, bow to me, discipline your self toward me, and you will reach me!
>
> —Bhagavad Gita 9.30–32, 34[16]

We have seen above how women poet-saints like Mirabai became famous for their all-consuming devotion to God, a devotion that in some cases superseded their more mundane wifely duties. Another such case is that of Mahadevi, the twelfth-century poet-saint and devotee of the god Siva, who in the following claims Siva as her true husband in contrast to human and mortal husbands who "die, decay":

> I love the Beautiful One
> > with no bond nor fear
> > no clan no land
> > no landmarks
> > for his beauty.
>
> So my lord, white as jasmine, is my husband.
> Take these husbands who die,
> > decay, and feed them
> > to your kitchen fires!
>
> Better than meeting
> > and mating all the time
> > is the pleasure of mating once
> > after being far apart.
>
> When he's away
> > I cannot wait
> > to get a glimpse of him.[17]

While occasionally women did emerge as leaders in various devotionalistic traditions of the Hindu religion, most commonly they participated in religious life in less public ways. Although excluded from the Hindu priesthood, women have always played important roles in religious festivals, ceremonies, and observances, both at home and in the temple. Among the religious practices that are especially common among Hindu women are various vows *(vrats)* and fasts. Such vows can be a means for developing yogiclike self-restraint; they are also undertaken as a kind of devotional act to a particular deity who is expected, in return, to grant certain boons: obtaining a good husband, fertility, protection for one's children and spouse, happiness for oneself and one's family, or just peace of mind.

The several purposes of undertaking religious vows are apparent in one contemporary Hindu woman's summary of the benefits of the vrat:

> One does *vrats* for purifying the mind, for steadying it, and to prevent the oscillating mind from becoming less strong. . . . A *vrat* is for giving peace of mind. It also gives peace to the senses, heart and intellect. It is for keeping away defilements of the mind. Through *vrats* we get assistance in regulating ourselves. We learn to control hunger, thirst and sleep. In this way we control our desires. . . . Some *vrats* are like this—they are observed for one's husband; some are observed for one's sons. Jivitputra, for instance, is observed when someone's child has not continued to live, or when a child dies immediately after childbirth. By performing this *vrat* their children will continue to live—good health will be maintained. Those who have none will get [offspring].[18]

## CONCLUSION

In present-day India, the ambivalence about women in general and particularly about women's participation in public and religious life continues. On the one hand, women in India are still subject to discrimination and inequality and are in some quarters plagued by practices such as child marriage, dowry deaths (where a newly wed wife is killed by her husband or his family for failure to produce the demanded dowry), and the poor treatment of widows. On the other hand, the percentages of Indian women in the professions compare favorably with those of the West; women are well represented in the medical and scientific pursuits, as well as in the arenas of politics and government.

The increasing participation of Hindu women in public, economic, and political life has in India, as elsewhere, also produced a kind of backlash. The recent rise of a Hindu nationalist movement has included an emphasis on a return of women to traditional roles as dutiful wives and mothers, as well as the use of gendered imagery to evoke feelings of protective patriarchy among Hindu men whose women are portrayed as threatened by various enemies and forces. For these Hindu nationalists, India itself is represented as an endangered woman ("Mother India") who must be guarded and defended from those who would defile her. Paradoxically, however, this attitude is sometimes voiced by women activists within the Hindu nationalist movement, women who have themselves assumed positions of leadership and public roles as professional spokespersons. Many of the women of this movement are trained in paramilitary skills and are independent and self-confident while, at the same time, acting as ideologues for a position that insists that Hindu women return to positions of subservience to men. Such contradictions are not unfamiliar to religious "fundamentalist" movements in other parts of the world where women have also assumed activist roles in the service of a reactionary ideology.

CHAPTER 5

# *Buddhism*

Ideals for women are generally of two sorts in the various Buddhist communities found around the world: those which acknowledge and indeed emphasize sexual difference and those which ignore gender in favor of a fundamental egalitarianism with respect to spiritual ability. The former type of ideal portrays women *as women* in socially defined roles as daughters, wives, and mothers. Such roles were primarily defined by a woman's association with men (their fathers, husbands, and sons) and thus a woman's moral identity came from her relationship to these men. Such socially defined roles were significantly shaped, of course, by local cultural practices and values, and since cultural diversity has always been a hallmark of the Buddhist world, there is naturally considerable difference between, say, Tibetan, Japanese, and Thai images of ideal women.

In contrast, the second type of Buddhist ideal for women is more concerned with individual spiritual attainment, especially in the achievement of states in which sexual difference is transcended. These ideals, more universalistic in perspective, tend to portray women as having the same access to the sources of the good life as men. These ideals, in which gender is necessarily and ultimately transcended, are not considered as deviations from the social ideals. They have been generally considered to be not just acceptable exceptions to those models of virtue defined by sexual difference, but actually superior to them. With their universalistic orientation, ideals of the second type also tend to be less affected by local cultural practices and values and thus they are commonly emphasized when Buddhism is introduced to new communities. This has been especially the case in the twentieth-century introduction of Buddhist thought and practice to Europe and North America, where universalist ideals have predominated and sometimes inspired critiques of inequalities stemming from an emphasis on sexual difference in defining social roles.

## MODELS OF VIRTUE FOR WOMEN AND SEXISM

This last point reminds us that although in theory these two types of ideals are quite distinct from one another, in practice there is usually some relationship between them. We must always carefully examine this relationship because each ideal has the potential of both supporting and undermining the other. We will see below, in the discussion of models of virtue for mothers, how images of ideals for women were used by men to define and cultivate their own universalist responsibility to others; that is, men used idealized images of mothers to cultivate religious states that ultimately transcended gender.

At the same time, as we see in the following exchange between a husband and wife from a medieval Japanese text, images of women in social roles could also be used—again by men—as evidence of why women were incapable of universalist religious roles and attainments. The account of the exchange is actually told by the wife after she has become a Buddhist nun, and we pick up her story at a point where she is explaining her desire to become enlightened once she realized the transience of everything about human life:

> On my way home an old skull lying in the grass by the roadside caught my eye. There was no reason to find this sight shocking, but the eyeless skull with some of its teeth missing and its sex indistinguishable reminded me of the verse:

> Skin-deep is the difference
> Between men and women.
> As skeletons we are all the same.

She took the skull home and placed it next to her husband's pillow. When he saw it as he awoke, he screamed and demanded to know what was the meaning of his wife's action. The wife explained:

> "You shouldn't be so surprised," I said. I took his hand again and had him feel my face at length. "What's the difference? This skull is only as different from my face as a frame with or without silk stretched over it. You must not have any feeling for me! However much a husband and wife care for each other, it's not a bond that lasts long. . . . It is true that we must inevitably suffer the pain of separation from our loved ones, it is a fact that we cannot avoid parting from whomever we may meet. You too must seek enlightenment."

We see in these comments of the wife a common Buddhist assumption that an orientation toward enlightenment is at odds with marital roles. Crucially, the wife insists to her husband that the suffering that comes when human relationships inevitably end empties them of value even when they are still intact, a suggestion profoundly significant not only for marriage but for all ideals for women defined by such relationships. The husband, however, resists his wife's aspirations to pursue enlightenment by saying: "However much you are motivated to seek enlightenment, you are a woman, and something will dim your fervor before long."[1]

The last comment by the husband reveals that the relationship between the two ideals can be and has often been marked by misogynist assumptions about women, assumptions that were common throughout the Buddhist world. These assumptions included the one found here, that women easily deviate from Buddhist ideals because of their natural dispositions, but it was also common among Buddhists (perhaps especially among male Buddhists?) to think that women, *because they are women,* are constitutionally incapable of achieving the highest goals of the Buddhist life.

The husband's comment reminds us that the attention to the sexual difference that underlies the ideals of women as daughters, wives, mothers, and widows rarely emphasized just difference. Indeed, sexual difference was all too easily interpreted as generating special burdens that women have to bear but men do not, as can be seen in the following passage from the Theravada canon:

> There are five unique sufferings which a woman experiences but men do not. What five? First, while still a girl, a woman goes to her husband's family in marriage without any of her own relatives. That is the first suffering that is experienced uniquely by women. Second, a woman menstruates. That is the second unique suffering. Third, a woman becomes pregnant. . . . Fourth, a woman experiences pain in labor. . . . Fifth, a woman has to wait upon a man. This is the fifth suffering experienced uniquely by women.[2]

This passage frames the biological differences between men and women—all having to do with reproduction—with androcentric cultural patterns that give frustration and pain to women. The effect is to suggest that the cultural patterns subordinating women to men are as inevitable as the biological differences. In a similar vein, another text in the Theravada canon says:

> There are five powers of a woman. What five? The power of beauty, the power of wealth, the power of family background, the power of sons, and the power of moral virtue. . . . Possessed of these five powers . . . women dwell confidently in a household . . .

[but] possessed of one power, a man continues to get the better of a woman. What power? The power of authority. Neither the power of her beauty, nor the power of her wealth, of her family background, nor her power of moral virtue can protect a woman who is mastered by the power of authority.[3]

Such ideas about the inevitable subservience of women with respect to men became so common and ordinary in Buddhist literature that Nichiren, an important thirteenth-century Japanese teacher, could say, "When I . . . read [Buddhist texts] other than the Lotus Sutra, I have not the slightest wish to become a woman." Moreover, we can also see from Nichiren that the social inequalities women endured were generally portrayed in Buddhist texts not as an unjust oppression of women, but as appropriate responses to their constituent nature: "One sutra condemns women as emissaries of hell. Another describes them as large snakes. Still another likens them to bent and twisted trees. And there is even a sutra that describes them as people who have scorched the seeds of Buddhahood. Buddhist scriptures are not alone in this regard; non-Buddhist writings also (disdain women)."[4]

This is not to say, however, that there have not been Buddhist critiques of such sexism. The nineteenth-century Chinese social activist T'an Ssu-t'ung, in fact, saw Buddhism as offering the resources to end the oppression of women in his country, but notice too how his critique of sexism ends up transcending sexual difference in a manner similar to what we heard the wife say above. In both cases, an equality between men and women is established by denying that there is any important difference between men and women.

> There is nothing to suggest men are superior to women. If we understand that both men and women are the basic components of heaven and earth, that they both have countless virtues and have

great things to do, that they are both equal, and have the same roles to perform in society, and that originally they were not born in the world for the sake of lust, then we should also know that "beautiful women" are simply made up of powder and clothes. When the powder and clothes are taken away, they are but flesh and blood, no different from us and having no feminine beauty that we can be fond of. With this understanding, we can then guide people so that men and women can have social intercourse; we can liberate them so that they can get used to each other, until they feel spontaneous in each other's company and mutually forget their differences, as in the mutual intercourse of friends; at that stage, they will not be conscious of the sex difference, let alone lust.[5]

The use of sexual difference against women is one of the less appealing, if not disturbing, aspects of social life. Buddhist history offers no exception to this, and thus critiques like that of T'an Ssu-t'ung are refreshing to find. Although sexual difference was routinely used against women in the Buddhist world, as elsewhere, this does not necessarily mean that ideals for women in the Buddhist traditions do not deserve our serious attention.

When we consider various models of virtue for women in the Buddhist traditions, our challenge is to go beyond both a simple and unreflective rejection of these ideals because of their association with misogynist attitudes and a naive attempt to appreciate the ideals without taking into account the broader social contexts in which they circulated and in which they often served as tools of oppression.

We can begin to meet this challenge by remembering that it is easy to mistake a substantial moral position for misogyny in many instances. For example, the idea that a woman's moral worth came from the quality of her relations with others seems, on the face of it, to be an attempt, as crude as it is sexist, to place limits on women's autonomy and self-control. Frequently, such notions did severely limit the ability of women to act freely in society, but in other significant ways the moral position that can be abstracted from such notions is still worthy of close consideration. For example, some aspects of Buddhist models of virtue for women could be taken as anticipating the work of the contemporary feminist moral theorist, Carol Gilligan, who has argued that women generally tend to see morality as primarily a sense of care and responsibility to particular others rather than as following abstract rules.[6] Moreover, this understanding of morality as arising out of given attachments to particular others is not one that Buddhists assumed was only true for women. It is a position that is recommended to both men and women, as is clear from the following story told by a twentieth-century Sri Lankan monk, one that is quite similar to the "Heinz dilemma"—the hypothetical problem about a man who must decide whether to steal medicine for his dying wife—which Gilligan and others have used to explore the processes of moral decision making:[7]

> A good, honest, hardworking villager falls ill with a fever. For some time he manages to get medication and feed his wife and children through his meager savings, but they were soon gone. . . . [That year] the crops are abundant [in his village], and the convalescing good man sends his child to get some cassava from the 40 acre garden of the village headman. The child is refused, and the desperate father steals some. Can a father resist when his two little children are withering of starvation while there is food within sight, even if stealing would send him to hell straight away?
> 
> The man is found guilty of theft, but the monk explains: It is true that stealing is a sin. It is true that monks should explain to their flocks the consequences of stealing. But this helpless fellow is not a thief. He is the most virtuous man in the village. He was tempted to steal because of the love of his children.[8]

When considering models of virtue for women in Buddhist literature we face a challenge similar to that faced by this monk in his little story about the father who steals food for his children: to find ways of distinguishing between what is wrong—whether it be stealing or sexism—and virtue.

## MODELS OF VIRTUE FOR WOMEN THROUGH THE LIFE CYCLE

We will look at models of virtue for women as daughters, wives, mothers, and in old age in this section. Giving attention to each of these social roles will necessarily make this section the longest in the chapter.

Buddhist images of daughters are the vaguest of the four. On the one hand, young girls are simply children, and they are considered to be basically the same as boys. The spontaneous activities of children's play bring pleasure and delight to their parents, who, "when they see their little children who have been playing outside come in with their bodies covered with dirt, they show their affection by cleaning off the dirt, stroking their heads and kissing them all over."[9] Similarly, daughters as well as sons are expected to be obedient and respectful toward their parents as they mature.

On the other hand, however, traditional models of virtue for daughters which are more detailed tend to portray them as training to become adults. Buddhists in the past were like many other premodern cultures in which a sense of childhood as an independent and distinctive stage of human life, with its own worth and contours, was barely acknowledged. Parents give their children training in the Buddhist morality, such as the Five Precepts (the basic morality recommended to all Buddhists), to equip them for a good life as an adult, and Buddhist texts did see these virtues as helpful to adult women: "Possessed of five things. . .women dwell confident at home. What five? A woman does not take life, from taking what is not given, from sexual misconduct, from lying, and from the use of intoxicants which give rise to sloth."[10]

For parents in Buddhist societies, training a girl to be an adult meant, in most respects, preparing her to become a wife. Conventional expectations can be seen in one of the Buddha's sermons from the Theravada canon where a layman asks the Buddha to advise his daughters:

> "Lord, these girls of mine will be going to their husbands' families; lord, let the Exalted One counsel them, let the Exalted One advise them, for their own good and happiness for many a day!" Then the Exalted One spoke to them and said:
> 
> "Wherefore, girls, train yourselves in this way: To whatsoever husband our parents shall give us—wishing our weal, seeking our happiness, compassionate, because of compassion, for him we will rise up early, be the last to retire, be willing workers, order all things sweetly and be gentle voiced. Train yourself thus, girls.
> 
> "And in this way also, girls: We will honour, revere, esteem and respect all whom our husband reveres, whether mother or father, recluse or godly man, and on their arrival will offer them a seat and water. Train yourself thus, girls.
> 
> "And in this way also girls: We will be deft and nimble at our husband's home-crafts, whether they be of wool or cotton, making it our business to understand the work, so as to do and get it done. Train yourself thus, girls.
> 
> "And in this way also, girls. Whatever our husband's household consist of—slaves, messengers and workfolk—we will know the work of each by what has been done, their remissness by what has not been done; we will know the strength and the weakness of the sick; we will divide the hard and soft food, each according to his share. Train yourself thus, girls.
> 
> "And in this way also, girls: The money, corn, silver and gold

that our husband brings home, we will keep safe watch and ward over it and act as no robber, thief, carouser, wastrel therein. Train yourself thus, girls."[11]

Diligence, energy, gentleness, and respect are all virtues that are highly valued in both men and women in Buddhist societies. Each is seen as a character trait that is helpful for anyone who is serious about making progress in the religious life delineated by the Buddha. The qualities of rising early, retiring late, energy, and gentle disposition, which are recommended to the girls, are all found in images of ideal monks; at the same time, however, these same character traits are also applied in Buddhist texts to the ideal servant or slave, a reminder that we must keep in view the broader social contexts in which models for women circulated if we are to take their measure accurately. Women, in their social roles, are frequently treated more like servants than monks, in so far as the social identities of women and servants are both defined by their relations with others, whereas this is less true of a monk.

We can see from the above passage that good daughters will be those who apply themselves to learning the skills and cultivating the character traits that will later make them good wives. Their personal happiness is traced to their willingness and ability to become responsible to and for others, most notably the men to whom they are related.

Let us turn now to another account of the ideal wife. This one is part of a long story, and the excerpt we will quote here is also long, but in its details, we glimpse a fuller picture of one traditional image of an ideal wife.

It comes from a *Jataka* collection, the stories that the Buddha told about his previous lives as he prepared to become a Buddha. This collection was well known in Sri Lanka and Southeast Asia, where the Theravada tradition is found. In this story, Mahosadha, the future Buddha in a previous life, goes in search of a bride disguising his wealth and noble position in society, a detail that suggests that while women could be a financial asset to a family, whether through their labor or their own resources, there may have been some wariness about women doing the same thing and marrying men "for money." Once he finds a suitable bride, however, Mahosadha mistreats her in horrific ways as a test to see if she has the right qualities to be his wife:

> Mahosadha disguised himself as a tailor, and without telling his friends, went alone to another town. An old merchant family that had fallen on hard times lived there. That family had a daughter named Amara who was beautiful, virtuous, and possessed every good characteristic imaginable. Early that morning she had decided to bring food to where her father was plowing, and she was going by the same road as Mahosadha. When the future Buddha saw her coming, he noticed all her good characteristics[12] and thought that if she was unmarried, then it would be good if she became his wife. She, in turn, saw him and thought that if she could live in the house of a man like this, then she could change her family's fortunes. The future Buddha thought that he could discover both her marital state and her intelligence with a hand-gesture. Standing at a distance, he made a fist. She knew that he was asking if she was married and she gestured back with an open hand. Understanding her, he came closer and asked her her name. She replied, "Sir, I am named after that which is not, never was, and never will be." He said, "Madam, your name must be Amara (literally: Deathless)." "That's right, Sir." "Madam, for whom are you carrying food?" "For the god of the eastern direction." "The gods of the east are mothers and fathers, so you must be bringing food to your father." "That's right, Sir." "What is your father doing?" "He is making one into two." "Ploughing is a way of making one into two, so he is ploughing right now." "That's right, Sir." "In what place is your father ploughing?" "The place of no re-

turn." "The place of no return is a cemetery. Your father must be ploughing near a cemetery." "That's right, Sir." "Will you come again today, Madam?" "If it comes, I will not come, but if it does not come, I will come." "I think your father is ploughing near a riverbank, and if the waters come, you will not come, but if they do not come, you will come." "That's right, Sir."

After such conversation, Amara offered him a drink from what she had prepared for her father. The future Buddha was reluctant to refuse and said that he would like a drink. Then she put down the jar carrying the liquid and the future Buddha thought that if she offered it without giving him water to wash his hands, then he would just leave. She, however, first brought water to wash the cup and also water for him to wash his hands. She then filled the cup with something to drink. It was a rice gruel, but it was very lumpy. The future Buddha asked why the gruel was so thick and she told him that the rice was grown during a dry season and thus still remained coarse when cooked. He drank the gruel and then rinsed his mouth, and when he was finished, he asked her to tell him the way to her house. She did so and then went with the remaining gruel to where her father was.

Amara returned home in the evening, carrying wood and leaves that she had gathered in the forest. She left them by the front door and entered in through the back door. Her parents then returned. The future Buddha then was invited to eat. She served him, then her parents before eating herself. She washed her parents' feet and the future Buddha's feet. For several days, he stayed there watching her. Then one day to test her he said, "Amara, take half a measure of rice and cook me gruel, a cake, and boiled rice." She did as asked, using large grains of rice to make gruel, middle-sized grains she boiled, and she made a cake with the little grains. She made appropriate foods to have with the gruel, cake, and boiled rice. She served the gruel to the future Buddha. He took a mouthful, and although it tasted wonderful, he spit it out and said to test her, "Why have you ruined my rice?

Don't you know how to cook?" She was not angry but just gave him the cake to eat. He did the same with that, and then with the rice too, saying, "If you didn't know how to cook, why did you waste my property?" Acting like he was angry, he mixed everything she had cooked together and dumped it over her head and ordered her to sit by the door. She did as she was told, and was agreeable, not angry at all. Knowing that she was without pride, he said, "Come here, Madam." She came as soon as she was spoken to.

When the future Buddha first came he had brought a thousand rupees and a dress in his bag. He took out this dress and gave it to her, telling her to bathe with her friends and after getting dressed, to come to him. The wise man gave her parents all the money he had brought or earned, and comforted them. He then took her back to the city with him. At the city, he began to test her again. He made her sit outside the gatekeeper's house, and told the gatekeeper's wife of his plans before he went to his own house. Then he called his own men, and gave them a thousand pieces of money to do what he said and test her.

They did as they were told. She refused their advances, saying, "That is not worth the dust on my master's feet." They came back and told what had happenened. He sent them again, and a third time, and then even a fourth time when he told them to grab her hands and bring her by force. They did as they were told, but when she saw the future Buddha, she did not recognize him surrounded as he was by wealth and splendor. She laughed and cried at the same time. He asked her the reason for each of these. She said that she laughed when she saw his magnificence, and thought that such wealth is not received without a reason, but must have been received because of some good deed done in a previous life. She also explained that she wept when she thought that he would now violate the property that was watched and guarded by another and that he would go to hell as a result. "Out of compassion for you I cried." After this test, he knew how pure a person she was, and he sent her back to the gatekeeper's house. Putting his tailor's disguise back on, he went to that house and spent the night with her.

He went to the palace the next day and told his mother how he found a bride. She told his father, who was king, and had Amara adorned with every ornament. She had her seated in a great carriage, and brought her with great honor to the future Buddha's house, amidst great celebration. The king sent the future Buddha a gift of a thousand pieces of money; all the citizens of the city sent gifts too. Amara divided all of these gifts into two parts and gave one part back to those who gave it, thus winning the hearts of the people. From that day the future Buddha lived with her in happiness.[13]

The horrible mistreatment of Amara at the hands of her husband, from the cruel tests of her character to the casual treatment of her as property, is probably the first thing that anyone notices about this story. And the approval of her servantlike behavior, especially when she enters the back door of the house instead of the front, is also disconcerting. It is worth remembering, however, that this is just a story, one told to make a point. Although the hyperbolic quality of the story serves our purposes here in so far as it starkly outlines a wide range of qualities that some Buddhists thought a wife should have, it should not be taken as a reflection of how Buddhist communities thought real women should be treated or as an indication of how Buddhist women actually were treated. In fact, one of the effects of this story of Amara's mistreatment may have been to force a reader to consider whether the admired qualities idealized in models of virtue for women actually contribute inadvertently to their mistreatment.

What are the qualities of a wife idealized in this story? We have already noted among the admired qualities of an ideal wife a sense of obedience to her husband, suggested here by how quickly and without complaint Amara accedes to his unreasonable demands, and her stewardship with respect to household finances, suggested by the frugal way that she uses rice to prepare in the most efficient way the three kinds of food he asks for. The story calls our attention to moral qualities that a wife should possess: she should be sexually faithful; gentle and without anger, even when provoked; without pride; respectful and attentive to her parents. Just as the Buddha advised the girls in the passage above, Amara rises early to cook food for her father and we can be sure that she goes to bed later than everyone else in the house.

There are a number of other things to consider in this story, all of which emphasize Amara's strengths. We should not overlook that the story assumes a basic equality between husband and wife in terms of intellect and character; it is also possible to say that, in terms of character, Amara is superior to her husband. Amara's intellect comes across in the flirtatious talk between her and the future Buddha. The depths of Amara's character emerge both in her forbearance toward the provocations of Mahosadha—when he humiliates her in public by smearing her body with food—and the compassion she displays when she both laughs and cries for the future Buddha when she mistakes him for a rapist. Forbearance is one of the highest virtues of the Buddhist life for both men and women, as we see in the following selection from Arya Sura's *Jatakamala*, a medieval Indian narrative collection:

> If... one is afraid of evil, one should take pains to avoid such corruption, by cultivating its opposite. Just as a fire, however fierce, is quenched when it meets a large river brimful of water, so a raging heart grows calm if one inclines to forbearance, that mainstay in this life and the next. Practice forbearance and you will avoid evil

by cutting it off at the root. The result will be that you arouse no ill feeling because of your friendly disposition. You will be loved and honored for it and thereby win happiness.[14]

Two other statements from Arya Sura's *Jatakamala* can help us see the significance of Amara's laughter and tears before the man she perceives as a potential rapist: Compassionate souls, who have great powers of judgment, are not so much troubled by the hardship they themselves experience as that which befalls others.[15] "[I]t is other people's suffering which makes good people suffer: it is that which they cannot endure, not their own suffering."[16]

The cultivation of compassion is a critical part of the pursuit of enlightenment, and the portrayal of Amara as more concerned for the well-being of her husband than for herself, despite all his provocations, displays the degree to which she has cultivated this important virtue. Compassion, in Buddhist understanding, is a universalist ideal, one that everyone in pursuit of enlightenment must cultivate to perfection. The story of Amara appears to be in agreement with the arguments of some contemporary feminist ethics that say that the socialization of women and their social roles in families, especially as mothers, incline women to be more oriented toward care for others in their moral lives.[17]

Before turning to Buddhist ideals for mothers, it is worth noting that many of the ideals for wives found in the story of Amara still have a wide currency in the Buddhist world, even in those global movements with fundamentally universalistic orientations, although obviously these ideals are not commended by portrayals of the mistreatment of women. For example, Daisaku Ikeda, the leader of Soka Gakkai International, a dynamic international Buddhist movement that originated in mid-twentieth-century Japan and is now found in 120 countries, recently spoke of his marriage in one of his weekly newspaper columns, which circulate among the Soka Gakkai membership:

> My wife knows the truth about me better than anyone, and I think I know her devotion and patience better than anyone else could. . . . Women tend to be more practical than men, and view everything with the strength of a realism rooted in daily life. No man can match a woman's keen intuition to see through to the essence of things, her depth of wisdom and her ability to take calm action. . . . Kaneko is never without a smile. And she is so optimistic that she often amazes me. She says "I've learned a lot, having gone with you through many hardships. And I've come to the point where I am never taken by surprise, no matter what happens."
>
> When we married, my teacher gave her the following advice: Whatever unpleasant things may fill your day, always send him—[Ikeda], that is—off and greet him back home with a smile. This may seem like very simple advice, but I think it has taken great reserves of strength and wisdom to put into practice every day, as Kaneko has done.[18]

Ikeda's last comment about his wife's "great reserves of strength and wisdom," both valued spiritual qualities, reminds us once again that Buddhist models of virtue for women often portray women as having exceptional moral and religious character traits *in their social roles*. While this does make an important connection between the two types of ideals for women found among Buddhists, it does have a cost. Rarely do we see the women in these models depicted as having the complex, if not contradictory, characters that most of us do in fact have. Thus the models do not acknowledge that women have "ups and downs," act generously as well as selfishly, are cruel as well as kind, love as well as hate, and do and are all of these things at the same time. This, of course, is in the nature of an ideal, but inevitably in communities using these models of virtue there will be a gap between ideal and real. That gap can both inspire and oppress.

Nowhere is a gap between idealization and realistic possibility more visible than in Buddhist models of mothers. The image of the long-suffering and self-sacrificing mother is one of the most emotive and common images in Buddhist ethics and it is widely applied in many contexts. The Buddha himself is commonly depicted as a mother and this is a good indication of the centrality of the image as a model of virtue in Buddhist cultures: "Like a mother who becomes calm when a child nurses and thinks, 'It's something good that he's getting when he takes milk from the breast,' so the Buddha becomes happy for others and thinks, 'I will win over the minds of the whole world, that is, all my children.'"[19]

The image of a mother is even applied to wives, as can be seen from the following example from the Theravada canon; note how the verse alludes to many of the qualities we saw in the story of Amara.

> Whoever with compassion always cares
> for her husband like a mother for her child
> and also guards his stored-up wealth,
> let her be called a mother as well as a wife.[20]

As mentioned above, the image of the mother is frequently used by men in their own spiritual practices, something which complicates how we understand these images as models of virtue for actual mothers. For example, the individual cultivating compassion and loving kindness is frequently urged to model her or his behavior on that of a mother, as we see in "The Loving-kindness Discourse," again from the Theravada canon:

As a mother with her life
Might guard her son, her only child,
Would he maintain unboundedly
His thought of love for all the world
He would maintain unboundedly,
Above, below, and all around,
Unchecked, no malice with or foe.[21]

The image of an idealized mother is also employed in meditations designed to overcome hostility toward others, through the recollection of the fact that the cruel enemy now has been a nurturing mother in a previous life. This meditation is found throughout the Buddhist world, but the following example is taken from Tsong-Kha-Pa (1357–1419), one of the greatest teachers in the Tibetan Buddhist tradition:

> Underlying the contemplation of all the beings as one's own mother, is the initial contemplation in regard to the mother of this life. One should think a single time, "I contemplate in front the clear image of my mother"; and should think, "The present time is not all: since beginningless life cycles the count of my mothers pass beyond all calculation. Thus in her time in the mother role she protected me against all harm, provided me with all benefit and happiness. In particular in this life also, the first thing I did was take a long period in her womb. Thereafter, in the time of rearing, my downy baby hair pressed against her warm flesh. Her ten fingers gave me recreation. She suckled me with the milk from her breast. With her mouth she fed me. My snivel she wiped from my mouth. Wiping away with her hand my filth, she succored me wearilessly by diverse means. Moreover, my own capacity falling short, she gave me food and drink in the time of hunger and thirst; clothes when I shivered; money when I was 'broke.' Even when those necessities were not found easily, nevertheless, mixing

with sin, suffering, and evil reports, she served, rearing me to the utmost of her ability." Where there are such things as disease and pain in a son, she thinks, "Better I die than my son die; better I be sick than my son be sick; better I suffer than my son suffer." She chooses this course sincerely; then provides the means of dispelling (those things, suffering, etc.).[22]

It is important to keep in mind that such idealizations are used in spiritual practices that are not directly concerned with the moral development of women *as women*. In other words, they are images of virtuous women that are used for other purposes than as ideals for women, but the idealizations will, in fact, affect models of virtue for women. In the meditation above, the image of the ideal mother, who suffers and sacrifices on behalf of the son, is used to generate universal compassion, an ideal that is presumed to transcend sexual difference. At the same time, the image of the ideal mother is not easily distinguished from expectations for real-life mothers.

We can see that similar idealizations of mothers play a role in even a son's memories of his actual mother. A medieval Chinese text, *The Sutra on the Profound Kindness of Parents*, lists a number of actions a mother did for a son:

> Giving birth to this [son's] body,
> Swallowing the bitter and spitting out the sweet [for the baby to eat],
> Cleaning up the filth—
> She is not afraid of the hard work.
> Suffering hot and cold,
> She never shrinks from hardship.
> Putting the son in the dry places [in the bed]
> And sleeping on the wet spots herself.
> And for three years,
> [Giving] him her "white blood" to drink.[23]

It is worth noting that both of these models are organized around "memories" of the nursery, but they are memories that probably no one can directly have. None of us remembers being nursed by our mothers or having our diapers changed. These models of virtue cannot be challenged by objecting that "my mother" was not like that; although, realistically, probably every mother at one time or another is not like this ideal. The model, however, is intended to generate feelings of gratitude and obligation in the child, feelings which in turn will motivate appropriate reciprocal actions.

In other contexts, however, Buddhists depict the memories of mothers themselves quite differently, and typically their memories are defined by loss and especially by the death of children. To be a mother in Buddhist literature is commonly to be the mother of a dead child, as can be seen in the following passage from the "awakening story" of a Zen nun:[24]

> The day I can never forget arrived! May 7, 1945: while I still held in my hands the news of my son's death in battle, his remains were ceremoniously delivered. The agony and grief I felt as I held in my arms the small box of plain wood cannot be expressed with such phrases as "I felt like vomiting blood," or "my heart was broken." Only another mother who has experienced it can know.
>
> I was pushed from a world of light into a world of gloom. I lost all desire to live; every bit of happiness was taken away in grief and hopelessness.[25]

Such experiences of grief and hopelessness, however, were sometimes transformed, through Buddhist practice, into a sense of freedom and peace, qualities that are just as much at the pinnacle of the Buddhist life as compassion. Thus the Zen nun quoted above came to a very different experience through her practice of a particular style of meditation; in the following passage there is an allusion to her meditation in the word *Mu*, the answer to a question about whether a dog has the capacity of being a Buddha:

> From everywhere I could hear wonderful, indescribable music. Was this a visit to the paradise of the Pure Land? I didn't know, but it was the greatest of joys. No longer was there either a corrupt and troublesome world nor an honored teacher. My clinging to my beloved son vanished, and the painful search for *Mu* also disappeared in this ecstatic, exalted state of mind.[26]

Buddhist difficulties with perceiving women as persons in their own right and not in social relationships to men are apparent when we consider women in the last stages of the life cycle, although women in this stage of life are more an exception to the rule. Frequently in Buddhist societies older women are seen as quite different from younger women; in some cultures (Thailand, for example), postmenopausal women are sometimes considered as having a different gender from younger women. Moreover, older women share many qualities with elderly men. There are significant exceptions, of course. Prestige and respectability are qualities of both elderly men and women, and, in important instances, the contributions of elderly women to society are highly valued. For example, in Thailand, elderly married women who are not widowed, separated, or divorced play a key role in marriage ceremonies. They symbolize established, stable marriages, and as such, they are capable of giving their blessings to younger people.

At the same time, however, the most significant fact of an older person, aging, is not gendered. Rather aging displays to a person the processes of impermanence that are the condition of human suffering more generally. Portrayals of elderly women depict them as having experiences of freedom transcending gender through the experience of aging itself, as can be seen in the following verse by an elderly nun:

> I wandered for alms.
> I leaned on a stick.
> My whole body was weak
> and trembled.
> Suddenly I fell down
> and could see clearly
> the misery of this body.
> My heart was freed.[27]

## DEVIATIONS FROM THE IDEAL

Women who become nuns in the Buddhist world in old age generally do so either in response to the common processes of impermanence or because they are in need of care and protection because they have no relations to support them. But it would be extremely misleading to leave the impression that the Buddhist monastic life has an appeal only to older women. Younger women also join the monastic order for the same reasons as older women, out of a profound sense of the unsatisfactory nature of the conventional world or out of a desire to be free from the constraints of that world. We can see this awareness that it is imperative to live life in another way and this sense of a profound opposition between life in the Buddhist monastic order and the everyday life of a layperson in the following statement by Aoyama, a contemporary Japanese nun:

> Renunciation is a 180 degree transformation of the value of things. If there is only money, one feels that all happiness is possible, so one runs around to obtain money. However, the world is not that well designed. Human beings, gratefully, are not made that way.
>
> Even when one's every wishes are granted just as one likes, those with a heart will hear the wind in the depth of their breast. Once one senses this doubt, those who hear the sound of this wind will hear it evermore. This is the gate to religiosity. Renunci-

ation is the form of those who understand this gate. Renunciation is the form of those who seriously understand the joy of truth.

People think of themselves as adorable. For one's whole lifetime one will not change. But no one knows when it will end. Everyone wants to live to the fullest and live without regrets. People who renunciate are resolved to being happy. Nuns do not abandon the world, rather, we clearly recognize this world with respect. It is not casting off the world, but understanding unequivocally the genuine joy of this world. This is renunciation.[28]

Because being a nun was always a valued alternative to the social roles of wife and mother, women also became nuns in order to avoid or escape marriage. As shown by the following song about Guanyin, sung by a Chinese Buddhist pilgrim, this motivation could be quite explicit:[29]

> I ask the Buddhas of the ten directions:
> Which road leads to spiritual cultivation?
> In the west, there is no other than King Miaozhuang.[30]
> There is truly a chaste woman in the household of
>   King Miaozhuang.
> First, she does not have to bear the ill humor of her
>   parents-in-law.
> Second, she does not have to eat the food of her husband.
> Third, she does not have to carry a child in her womb or
>   on her arms.
> Fourth, she does not need a maid to serve her.
> Every day she enjoys peace and quiet in her fragrant room.
> Turning over the cotton coverlet, she sleeps on the bed alone.
> Stretching out her legs, she went into the Buddha hall.
> Pulling in her feet, she withdrew into the back garden.[31]
> For the sake of cultivation, she suffered punishment by
>   her parents.
> But now, sitting on the lotus throne, she enjoys blessings.[32]

Generally, in Buddhist monasticism one's motivations for entering the order mattered less than what one did once one was ordained. Above all, one was expected to be celibate. A diverse set of rules regulated external practice in considerable detail. Monastic regulations addressed where one could live and with whom, what one could wear and how one could get clothing, when and what one could eat, and the use of money; any deviation from these regulations could result in punishment or expulsion from the monastic order. Such detailed regulations inevitably meant that the monastic life itself did not embody freedom; rather, it was seen as the means to the attainment of ultimate freedom. The structure and disciplined nature of daily life in a contemporary Japanese Zen convent makes this clear:

| | |
|---|---|
| 4:00 A.M. | wake up |
| 4:15 | meditation |
| 5:00 | morning chanting of Buddhist scriptures |
| 6:15 | cleaning of nunnery |
| 7:30 | breakfast |
| 8:00–12:00 | classes, working together, or private study |
| 12:00 | lunch |
| 12:30–3:00 | classes, working together, or private study |
| 3:00 | tea |
| 4:00 | evening chanting of Buddhist scriptures |
| 4:30 | cleaning worship hall |
| 5:30 | dinner, consisting of day's leftovers |
| 6:00–8:00 | private study in one's own room |
| 8:15 | nightly meditation |
| 9:00 | lights out[33] |

Note how many of the same virtues which we saw commended to wives seem implicit in this daily schedule: diligence, frugality, obedience, and attentiveness to tasks at hand.

Women did not completely escape subservience to men by

becoming members of the monastic order. Buddhist tradition remembers the Buddha as establishing a monastic community for women with only the greatest reluctance, and when he did, he imposed a number of special rules for women. These included:

> A nun, even one who has been ordained for a hundred years, must respectfully salute a monk, even one who has been ordained but a day. . . .
> It is forbidden for nuns to criticize monks for real or nonexistent offenses; it is not forbidden for monks to criticize nuns for real offenses. . . .
> Nuns should not receive food, beds, seats, or lodging ahead of monks . . . .
> Every fortnight on festival days, the nuns should approach the community of monks and ask them for instruction.[34]

Throughout Buddhist history there have been debates over the significance of such rules, and what they say about the spiritual status of women, but at the same time, the Buddhist monastic order has frequently been the venue for women to enjoy a degree of social freedom that was generally denied their lay counterparts.

## WOMEN AND PUBLIC LIFE

As we have seen throughout this chapter, models of virtue for women are frequently taught and discussed in Buddhist communities by means of examples. This is especially the case with models for women in public life. In this section, we will look at three examples of women in Buddhist public life, although admittedly many others could have been chosen for each of the distinct social roles they represent. One is a married woman who was an exemplary patron of the Buddhist monastic order during the lifetime of the Buddha; one is a lay religious teacher from twentieth-century Thailand; and the last is a thirteenth-century Zen master who was the founder of a network of monasteries.

Our first example is known as Visakha, and her example is best known in the Theravadin traditions of Sri Lanka and Southeast Asia. She is described in the Theravada canon as chief among the female lay disciples of the Buddha and as an ideal lay woman. She is sometimes described through her son as Migara's mother, an illustration of how women's identity often came from their relationships with men, but her example also suggests the considerable independence that women could achieve in public life as women. A sermon that the Buddha gave to her on one occasion shows this, with its reference to the power that women could win in this world and the next, although it does emphasize that her success in this world comes from her stewardship of a woman's husband's wealth; the language used here is identical to that which we saw in the advice to daughters above. The sermon also shows how roles in public life, such as work and religious roles, were casually interconnected with personal qualities and virtues:

> Endowed with four qualities, Visakha, women win power in this world; this world is in their grasp. With what four?
> 
> Herein, Visakha, a woman is capable at her work, she manages the servants, in her ways she is lovely to her husband, she guards his wealth.
> 
> And how, Visakha, is a woman capable at her work?
> 
> Whatever her husband's home industries, whether in wool or cotton, therein she is deft and nimble; gifted with an inquiring mind into all such undertakings, she is able to arrange and carry them out....
> 
> And how does she manage the servants?

Whatever her husband's household consists of . . . she knows the work of each . . . she knows the strength and the weakness of the sick; she divides the . . . food, each according to his share. . . .

And how is she lovely in her ways to her husband?

What her husband reckons to be unlovely, that she would not commit for very life's sake. . . .

And how does she guard his wealth?

Whatever money, corn, silver or gold her husband brings home, she keeps it secure. . . .

Endowed with these four qualities, Visakha, women win power in this world, this world is in their grasp.

Endowed with four qualities, Visakha, women win power in the next world, the next world is in their grasp. With what four?

Herein, Visakha, a woman is accomplished in faith, virtue, generosity, and wisdom.

And how is she accomplished in faith?

She has faith and believes in the enlightenment of the Buddha. . . .

And how is she accomplished in virtue?

She abstains from taking life, from stealing, from sexual misconduct, from lying, and from drinking liquor, the cause of sloth.[35]

And how is she accomplished in generosity?

She dwells at home with heart purged of the stain of avarice, given over to generosity, open-handed, delighting in giving, yoke-mate to asking,[36] she finds joy in almsgiving.

And how is she accomplished in wisdom?

She is wise and is endowed with wisdom into the way of the rise and fall of things, accomplishing the path to the complete destruction of suffering.[37]

Visakha is generally portrayed as a model of Buddhist generosity. She is said to have fed five hundred monks daily. Each day, she would go to hear the Buddha preach his afternoon sermon, and at its conclusion she would ask him if there was anything that he or his disciples needed. On one occasion she requested that the Buddha permit her eight things: that as long as she lived, she be allowed to (1) give robes to monks and nuns of the Buddha's monastic order; (2) feed whatever monks who came to her city; (3) give them provisions when they left; (4) give food to those members of the monastic order who were sick; (5) give food to those who take care of the sick; (6) give medicine for the sick; (7) give rice gruel (a nourishing food) to anyone needing it; and (8) give bathing robes to Buddhist nuns so that they might guard their modesty. The Buddha granted her all of these requests.

We can note two things about this portrayal of Visakha in public life. First, efforts on behalf of others are key to her identity and success in the world, a theme that we have already seen again and again in Buddhist models of virtue for women as women. Second, although her generosity toward the monastic order is said to be a key to her well-being in future lives, we should not overlook the ways in which it also contributes to her public success in this world. Anyone, male or female, who is generous with material assistance to the monastic order will be admired by others in a Buddhist society.

Being a generous donor to the monastic order is the most common public role that is recommended to laywomen for emulation, but it is not the only role possible. Any woman who undertakes religious practices such as meditation for her own spiritual welfare and then teaches what she discovers will be admired by others much more than a woman who is only concerned with the welfare of others.[38] While less common, it is thus possible for a woman to become a respected religious teacher in her own right. This possibility, however, is not grounded in any preexisting social role. Each woman who assumes it creates that public role anew and for herself through the religious attainments personally won by her through her own cultivation and practice.

One woman who created such a position for herself is Upasika (female lay disciple) Kee Nanayon (1901–1978), a woman who began to teach publicly in Thailand in the 1950s. Kee Nanayon had made a resolution when she was young not to get married, and in her early forties she established a religious retreat with an aunt and uncle at which she devoted herself to the practice of meditation. When she began to teach, her message was entirely out of her practical experience; she never had her own meditation teacher nor did she follow a standardized course of study in Buddhist thought. Still word spread about the seriousness of her religious practice, practice through which she attained "wisdom into the way of the rise and fall of things, accomplishing the path to the complete destruction of suffering,"[39] one of the qualities that the Buddha commended to Visakha. As the value of her religious talks became known, more and more people began to visit her retreat center to hear her. Soon her talks were printed for wider distribution.

Kee Nanayon addressed herself to both men and women, concentrating on those ideals of the Buddhist religious life that transcend sexual difference. This, of course, put her outside the conventions of everyday social life, with their established roles for both men and women, but, like Aoyama, the Japanese Zen nun quoted above, she is quite self-conscious that this is the very foundation of the religious life:

> We've gone astray for far too long already, our lives almost gone after how many decades. Now we've come here to turn ourselves around. No matter how old you are, the air you breathe isn't just for your convenience and comfort, but for you to learn about suffering and stress. That way you'll be able to disband it. Don't

imagine that your family and relatives are essential to you. You are alone. You came alone and you'll go alone. . . . So isn't it worthwhile to strive for release? After all, it's something each of us has to find for him or herself. . . .

Reading yourself, contemplating yourself, you see new angles, you gain more precise self-knowledge each step of the way. It's not a question of being really expert about things outside. You see how what's inside is really inconstant, really stressful, really not-self. The way you used to fall for things and latch onto them was because of your blindness, because you didn't understand. So who can you blame? Your own stupidity, that's who—because it wanted to brag about how much it knew.

Now you know that you've still got a lot of stupidity left and that you'll have to get rid of it before you die. Every day that you still have breath left to breathe, you'll use it to wipe out your stupidity rather than to get this or be that or to dance around.[40]

Kee Nanayon's last comments can be taken as a searing indictment of the qualities embodied by Visakha, oriented as they were around "getting this" and "being that." Kee Nanayon would appear to have no interest in winning power in this world, or to have it in her grasp. But note how she transcends such interests by transcending the world structured by notions of sexual difference.

A similar transcendence of sexual difference is seen in the life of Mugai Nyodai, the Zen abbess who lived from 1223 to 1298.[41] Although she lived seven centuries ago, we can glimpse something of what must have been her presence during life from a life-size statue of her; it was the practice in medieval Japan to prepare a statue of a Zen teacher to serve as a proxy, an inspiration, to his (or her) disciples after his death. Mugai Nyodai's statue, when seen among statues of her male counterparts seems unremarkable: in her robes, with her head shaved, she seems more like the male Zen priests than her female contemporaries. But this is the important point. The highest public roles to which women could aspire in Buddhist societies often required them to renounce their identity as women, but women who assumed such roles were given, like their male counterparts, a license for independence and creativity.

We can see this license for freedom in Mugai's life. She was born into an elite family, was well educated, and had been married to a member of a politically well-connected clan; curiously, her biographies are quite vague or inconsistent about the men in her life, seemingly to emphasize her independence as a person. For reasons that are unclear to us, she began to study Zen—that is, to practice meditation—with a Chinese Zen master in middle age. Before his death, her teacher recognized her as his true student, an heir to his teachings. After her teacher's death, Mugai founded a temple in which she taught and ordained her own female students, and her efforts gradually produced a network of temples and convents that all looked to her for leadership; these temples were of considerable significance, religiously and economically, during her own lifetime.

In considering the lives of Kee Nanayon and Mugai Nyodai, we return again to some of the paradoxes of Buddhist models of virtue for women. The highest and most admired positions women could attain in Buddhist societies were ones in which women renounced their identity as women and became more like their male counterparts: sexless, celibate, and transcending all social relations defined by sexual difference, they achieved a spiritual equality with men. Curiously, these male counterparts, themselves aspiring to the same things as these women, to the highest attainments that the Buddhist life could offer, modeled themselves after the social roles that their female counterparts felt they had to leave behind, especially when they used the image of a mother who cares for her only child as a model for their own ethical lives as embedded in relationships of care and responsibility, rather than free from them.

But perhaps this is the greatest lesson to be drawn from Buddhist models of virtue for women: that models of virtue for women *as women* are also important models of virtue for men *as human beings*.

LITERARY SOURCES OF THE
WORLD RELIGIONS

## JUDAISM

Judaism, the religion, identifies as its authoritative source "the Torah," or "the teaching," defined as God's revelation to Moses at Sinai. Writings deemed canonical enter the category of Torah, though into that same category also fall all authentic teachings of every age. The revelation myth of Judaism maintains that at Sinai God revealed the Torah in two media, written and oral. That is to say, while part of the revelation took written form, another part was formulated orally and transmitted through memorization. The tradition of Sinai may then come to concrete expression through any great sage's teaching. But the account of the position of Judaism set forth in these pages derives from the dual Torah, written and oral, as set forth in the Hebrew Scriptures and as interpreted by "our sages of blessed memory," the rabbis of the first seven centuries of the Common Era.

### The Written Part of the Torah

We know the written part of the Torah as the Hebrew Scriptures of ancient Israel, or the "Old Testament." This is made up of the Pentateuch, or Five Books of Moses (Genesis, Exodus, Leviticus, Numbers, and Deuteronomy); the Former Prophets (Joshua, Judges, Samuel, and Kings); the Latter Prophets (Isaiah, Jeremiah, and Ezekiel); The Twelve Minor Prophets; and the Writings (Psalms, Proverbs, Job, Song of Songs (aka the

Song of Solomon), Ruth, Lamentations, Ecclesiastes, Esther, Daniel, Ezra, Nehemiah, and Chronicles). All translations from the written Torah come from the Revised Standard Version of the Bible.

### The Oral Part of the Torah: The Mishnah, Tosefta, and Two Talmuds

Judaism identifies a philosophical law code called the Mishnah (c. 200 C.E.) as the first and most important of the finally transcribed components of the oral Torah. The Mishnah is a set of rules in six parts, made up of laws dealing with the hierarchical classification of holy Israel in these categories: (1) agricultural life; (2) the holy calendar, Sabbaths, and festivals; (3) women and family; (4) civil law and the administration of justice and the state; (5) the Temple and its offerings; (6) purity laws. A tractate, or compilation of teachings, called Abot, "the Fathers," attached to the Mishnah, commences, "Moses received Torah at Sinai and handed it on to Joshua, Joshua to elders, and elders to prophets. And prophets handed it on to the men of the great assembly," and onward down to the very authorities of the Mishnah itself. That is how the document is placed within the oral tradition of Sinai. In addition to the Mishnah, three other writings carry forward the legal tradition of Sinai: the Tosefta (c. 300 C.E.), a set of further legal traditions in the model of those in the Mishnah; the Talmud of the Land of Israel (c. 400 C.E.), a systematic amplification of thirty-nine of the Mishnah's sixty-two topical tractates; and the Talmud of Babylonia (c. 600 C.E.), a commentary to thirty-seven of the same. The two Talmuds treat in common the second, third, and fourth divisions of the Mishnah. The former takes up the first; the latter, the fifth; and neither addresses the sixth. In addition, tractate Abot receives its Talmud in a compilation, the Fathers according to Rabbi Nathan, of indeterminate date.

## The Oral Part of the Torah: Midrash-Compilations

The work of commenting on the Mishnah and its legal traditions found its counterpart, among the same sages or rabbis, in the labor of commenting on books of the written Torah. This work produced Midrash, or exegesis, meaning the interpretation of Scripture in light of contemporary events by appeal to a particular paradigm, or pattern, that showed how Scripture imposed meaning on contemporary occasions. Those biblical books selected for intensive amplification are the ones read in the synagogue: Genesis, in Genesis Rabbah (c. 400 C.E.); Exodus, in Mekhilta Attributed to Rabbi Ishmael (of indeterminate date but possibly c. 350 C.E.); Leviticus, in Sifra (c. 350 C.E.), and also in Leviticus Rabbah (c. 450 C.E.); Numbers, in Sifré to Numbers; and Deuteronomy, in Sifré to Deuteronomy (both c. 350 C.E.). In addition, Midrash-Compilations serve four of the scrolls read in synagogue worship: Lamentations, read on the 9th of Ab to commemorate the destruction of the Temple; Esther, read on Purim; Song of Songs, read on Passover; and Ruth, read on Pentecost. The Mishnah, Tosefta, Talmuds, and Midrash-Compilations together form the authoritative canon of Judaism in its formative age, the first seven centuries of the Common Era. All translations of portions of the oral Torah in this book come from those made by the author.

## CHRISTIANITY

The Christian faith understands itself to be grounded in the Holy Spirit, God's self-communication. Access to the Holy Spirit is possible because in Jesus Christ God became human. The Incarnation (God becoming flesh, *caro* in Latin) is what provides the possibility of the Divine Spirit becoming accessible to the human spirit.

Speaking from the perspective of Christian faith, then, there is a single source of theology: the Holy Spirit, which comes from the Father and Son. But the inspiration of the Holy Spirit has been discovered and articulated by means of distinct kinds of literature in the history of the church. By becoming aware of the diversity of those sources, we can appreciate both the variety and the coherence of Christianity.

The Scriptures of Israel have always been valued within the church, both in Hebrew and in the Greek translation used in the Mediterranean world. (The Greek rendering is called the Septuagint, after the seventy translators who were said to have produced it.) Those were the only scriptures of the church in its primitive phase, when the New Testament was being composed. In their meetings of prayer and worship, followers of Jesus saw the Scriptures of Israel "fulfilled" by their faith: their conviction was that the same Spirit of God that was active in the prophets was, through Christ, available to them.

The New Testament was produced in primitive communities of Christians to prepare people for baptism, to order worship, to resolve disputes, to encourage faith, and for like purposes. As a whole, it is a collective document of primitive Christianity. Its purpose is to call out and order true Israel in response to the triumphant news of Jesus' preaching, activity, death, and Resurrection. The New Testament provides the means of accessing the Spirit spoken of in the Scriptures of Israel. Once the New Testament was formed, it was natural to refer to the Scriptures of Israel as the "Old Testament."

The Old Testament is classic for Christians because it represents the ways in which God's Spirit might be known. At the same time, the New Testament is normative: it sets out how we actually appropriate the Spirit of God, which is also the spirit of Christ. That is why the Bible as a whole is accorded a place of absolute privilege in the Christian tradition: it is the literary source from which we know both how the Spirit of God has been known and how we can appropriate it.

The term "Early Christianity" designates the time between

the second and the fourth centuries of the Common Era, the period during which the church founded its theology on the basis of the scriptures of the Old and New Testaments. Although Christians were under extreme—sometimes violent—pressure from the Roman Empire, Early Christianity was a time of unique creativity. From thinkers as different from one another as Bishop Irenaeus in France and Origen, the speculative teacher active first in Egypt and then in Palestine, a common Christian philosophy began to emerge. The period of Early Christianity might also be called a "catholic" phase, in the sense that it was characterized by a quest for a "general" or "universal" account of the faith, but that designation may lead to confusion with Roman Catholicism at a later stage, and is avoided here.

After the Roman Empire itself embraced Christianity in the fourth century, the church was in a position to articulate formally its understanding of the faith by means of common standards. During this period of Orthodox Christianity, correct norms of worship, baptism, creeds, biblical texts, and doctrines were established. From Augustine in the West to Gregory of Nyssa in the East, Christianity for the first and only time in its history approached being truly ecumenical.

The collapse of Rome under the barbarian invasions in the West broke the unity of the church. Although the East remained wedded to the forms of Orthodoxy (and accepts them to this day), the West developed its own structure of governance and its own theology, especially after Charlemagne was crowned as emperor of the Romans by Pope Leo III on Christmas Day in 800 C.E.

To severe arguments regarding political jurisdiction, East and West added doctrinal divisions. The pope was condemned in 876 by a synod in Constantinople for failing to stop a small change in the wording of the Nicene Creed, which has become accepted in the West. A papal legate in 1054 excommunicated the patriarch of Constantinople. Even that act pales in comparison with what happened in 1204: European Crusaders on their way to Jerusalem sacked and pillaged Constantinople itself.

European Christianity flourished during the Middle Ages, and Scholastic theology was a result of that success. The Scholastics were organized on the basis of educational centers, Thomas Aquinas at the University of Paris during the thirteenth century being the best example. During the periods of Early Christianity and Orthodoxy, theologies as well as forms of discipline and worship were developed for the first time. Scholastic theology was in the position of systematizing these developments for the usage of the West. At the same time, Scholastic theologians also rose to the challenge of explaining Christian faith in the terms of the new philosophical movements they came into contact with.

The Reformation, between the sixteenth and the eighteenth centuries, challenged the very idea of a single system of Christianity. Martin Luther imagined that each region might settle on its own form of religion. In England the settlement was on a national basis, while in John Calvin's Geneva the elders of the city made that determination. But in all its variety, the Reformation insisted that the Bible and worship should be put into the language of the people, and that their governance should be consistent with their faith.

From the eighteenth century until the present, Christianity in its modern form has been wrestling with the consequences of the rise of rationalism and science. The results have been diverse and surprising. They include Protestant Fundamentalism—a claim that the Bible articulates certain "fundamentals" which govern human existence—and the Roman Catholic idea of papal infallibility, the claim that the pope may speak the truth of the church without error. In both cases, the attempt is made to establish an axiom of reason that reason itself may not challenge. But modern Christianity also includes a vigorous acceptance of the primacy of individual judgment in the life of communities: examples include the Confessing Church in Germany, which opposed the Third Reich, and the current movement of Liberation Theology in Central and South America.

Today Christians may use many combinations of the sort of sources named here to articulate their beliefs, and the resulting pattern is likely to be as distinctive as what has been produced in the past.

## ISLAM

### The Qur'an

The single source that constitutes the basis of all inquiry into the religion of Islam is the Qur'an. Revealed to the Prophet Muhammad from 610 to 632 C.E., it is understood as God's own speech. That is to say, Muslims believe that the Qur'an is not merely inspired by God, it is exactly what God meant to say to the early Muslim community and to the world in general. Furthermore, God spoke to Muhammad (usually through the angel Gabriel) in Arabic, and to this day Muslims resist translation of the Qur'an into any other language. The Qur'an is about as long as the Christian New Testament. It is divided into 114 chapters (called *suras*), which range in size from a few verses to a few hundred. All but one of these suras begins with an invocation, "In the name of God, the Merciful, the Compassionate," and with these words pious Muslims begin all endeavors of importance. There are many translations of the Qur'an into English; that of A. J. Arberry is widely recognized as the best and is used in this series, despite the unfortunate gender bias in Arberry's language.[1]

The Qur'an describes itself as a continuation and perfection of a tradition of revelation that began with the Torah, revealed to the Jews, and the Gospels, revealed to the Christians. In fact, the Qur'an directly addresses Jews and Christians, urging them to put aside their differences and join Muslims in the worship of the one, true God: "Say: People of the Book! Come now to a word common between us and you, that we serve none but God" (The House of Imran. 3:56). Jesus and Moses are explicitly recognized as prophets, and the rules and pious regulations in the Qur'an fit in well with similar rules found in Judaism and Christianity. Of course, a special role is given to Muhammad, the seal of the prophets and the leader of the early Muslim community.

### *Sunna:* The Prophet as Text

The Prophet Muhammad serves as the second "text" for Muslims. Unlike the Qur'an, which is the single source for God's divine word in Islam, the words and deeds of the Prophet are found in many different sources. When it comes to the Prophet, precise words are not as important as his general "way of doing things"; in Arabic, this is called the Prophet's *sunna.*

The Prophet Muhammad ibn 'Abd Allah was born almost six centuries after Jesus' birth, around 570 C.E., and for the first forty years of his life he organized trading caravans. Around the year 610, he began meditating in a cave near his hometown of Mecca. During these meditations he was overwhelmed by a vision of the angel Gabriel commanding him, "Recite!" This event changed his life forever and he began, slowly, to preach to his relatives and neighbors. After years of effort, Muhammad and a small group of followers moved to the town of Medina. This *Hijra,* the emigration of Muslims from Mecca to Medina in 622 C.E., marks the beginning of the Muslim calendar and was a turning point for the early community. In Medina, hundreds flocked to the new religion, and when the Prophet died in 632, he left behind thousands of believers. The survival of this early group is testified to by the almost one billion Muslims in the world today. Now, as then, Muslims see the Prophet as an example of the ideal believer. Muslims often name their boys after the Prophet, wear clothes like his, and try to live according to his precepts.

*Hadith:* Examples of the Prophet's Sunna

Muhammad's words and deeds were preserved and passed on from generation to generation in a form of oral transmission known as hadith. The Arabic word *hadith* means "story," and a typical hadith begins with a list of those from whom the story was received, going back in time to the Prophet. Following this list is the story itself, often an account of the Prophet's actions in a particular situation or the Prophet's advice on a certain problem. The list of transmitters is an integral part of the hadith; for example: "al-Qasim—'A'isha—The Prophet said . . ." Here, al-Qasim (an early legal scholar) transmitted this hadith from 'A'isha (one of the Prophet's wives), who heard it directly from the Prophet. These stories were quite popular among early generations of Muslims, but no one attempted to collect and organize them until over a hundred years after the Prophet's death. Two important early collections of hadith are those by al-Bukhari (d. 870) and Muslim ibn al-Hajjaj (d. 875). Hadith are also found in works of history and in commentaries on the Qur'an. It is worth emphasizing that Muslims do not believe that Muhammad was divine. A careful distinction was maintained between divine words, which originated with God and therefore were put into the Qur'an, and Muhammad's general advice to his community. Both sets of words were spoken by the Prophet, but the first were written down and carefully preserved, while the second were handed down through the more informal vehicle of hadith.

*Tafsir:* Commentary on the Texts

Today, as in previous ages, Muslims often turn directly to the Qur'an and hadith for guidance and inspiration, but just as often, they turn to commentaries and interpretations of these primary sources. These commentaries concern themselves with questions of grammar, context, and the legal and mystical implications of the text. They expand the original source, often collecting interpretations of many previous generations together. The results can be massive. The Qur'an, for instance, is only one volume, but a typical commentary can be twenty volumes or more. The importance of commentary in the Islamic tradition demonstrates that the Qur'an and sunna of the Prophet are not the only sources for guidance in Islam. Rather, Muslims have depended on learned men and women to interpret the divine sources and add their own teachings to this tradition. Therefore, these commentaries are valuable sources for understanding the religious beliefs of Muslims throughout the ages. Together with the Qur'an and hadith, they provide a continuous expression of Islamic religious writing from scholars, mystics, and theologians from over fourteen centuries.

## BUDDHISM

Upon examining the major bodies of sacred literature in Buddhism, it must first be noted that Buddhism does not define "canon" in the same sense that the Judaic, Christian, and Islamic religions do. First of all, scriptures comprising a Buddhist canon are not deemed authoritative on the basis of being regarded as an exclusive revelation granted to humans by a supreme divine being. In principle, the ultimate significance of a given scriptural text for Buddhists lies less in the source from whom it comes, or in the literal meanings of its words, than in its ability to generate an awakening to the true nature of reality. Texts are principally valued according to their ability to enable one to engage in practices leading to an enlightened state of salvific insight, which liberates one from suffering, although they can also be utilized to serve other vitally important if less ultimate purposes, such as the cultivation of compassionate ethics, explication of philosophical issues, and protection from obstacles to personal well-being. Buddhism is also distinctive in that it has never established any one body that has functioned in an equivalent manner to the Rabbinate on Episcopate charged with the determination of a single, fixed, closed list of authoritative works for the entire tradition. On a local level, Buddhist canons, based on the hermeneutical standard of privileging the realization of enlightenment over source and word, have tended to remain open (to varying degrees) to the inclusion of new scriptures over the course of history.

It should not be concluded that the factors discussed above have ever substantially limited the amount of sacred literature produced in Buddhism or have relegated scripture to a status less than primary in the religion's history. On the contrary, the various major Buddhist collections of scripture are extraordinarily voluminous in size and have continuously occupied a most highly revered place in the tradition as primary sources of teaching.2 Appeals to a scripture's provenance have indeed played a momentous role in Buddhist history, with a primary determinate of a text's canonicity being recognition of it as containing *buddha-vacana,* the "spoken word" of a Buddha, or enlightened being—usually Siddhartha Gautama or Shakyamuni Buddha (563–483 B.C.E.)—the Indian founder of the religion. To reiterate, one can be sure that the authority assigned to buddha-vacana is derived in part from its source, but what is of utmost import is its liberating power as an indicator of enlightened wisdom.

Insofar as we can determine it, the buddha-vacana, first transmitted shortly after the end of Shakyamuni Buddha's life by his main disciples, at first came to consist of two major sets of texts. The first set is known as Sutra, and it comprises the discourses of the Buddha (or in some cases of his disciples, but with his sanction), relating the events in his past and present lifetimes and his practical and philosophical teachings. The second set, known as the Vinaya, presents the ethical discipline and monastic rules that regulate the life of the *sangha,* or community, as they were laid down by the Buddha. Collectively, these two sets form the core of what is known as dharma, or Buddhist doctrine.

In addition, Buddhist canons include texts that provide further explanation and guidance in the Dharma, such as commentaries on the Sutras and Vinaya, treatises on philosophical topics, and ritual and meditative manuals. Broadly known as Shastra, or exegesis, this type of work derived its authority not from being buddha-vacana, but from being authored by those scholiasts, philosophers, and meditation masters who came to be regarded by later Buddhists as of the highest accomplishments and explicatory skills. Perhaps the most important genre of Shastra texts is the collections known as Abhidharma ("Further Dharma"), which consist of systematic analyses and classifications of doctrine composed by scholastic masters as early as three hundred years after the Buddha.

Despite general agreement among Buddhist traditions on the principle that the words of a Buddha and the further exegeses by great masters of philosophy and meditation are what constitute authority and canonicity, there has also been profound disagreement among these traditions about conceptions of what a Buddha is and what a Buddha teaches, and in turn about which masters best explicated the most efficacious and reliable means to liberation. In addition to such sectarian differences, various regional and linguistic divisions have contributed to the compilation of a number of separate canons. Thus, in speaking of the major sources of Buddhism that will inform these volumes, it is necessary to briefly identify the religion's major sectarian and regional divisions.

The Buddhist world today can be divided according to three major traditions, each of which traces its origins to developments in India, presently inhabits a more or less definable geographic region outside India and subscribes to a distinctive body of scriptural sources, which the followers regard as the most authentic version of the Dharma. The Theravada ("Teaching of the Elders") tradition was the first of the three to historically form a distinct community (fourth century C.E.), and today it continues to thrive in the countries of Sri Lanka, Thailand, Myanmar (Burma), Laos, and Cambodia. The Theravada corpus of scripture—known as the Tripitaka ("Three Baskets") because of its division into the three sections of Sutra, Vinaya, and Abhidharma, described above—was rendered into written form in the Pali language by Sri Lankan elders in the first century B.C.E., but its origins are traced back to a council convened shortly after the end of the Buddha's life in the early fifth century B.C.E., during which his leading disciples orally recited the Buddha's words and began committing them to memory. Theravadins regard their texts as conserving the Dharma as it was originally taught and practiced by Shakyamuni and his most accomplished followers, who are known as *arhats,* or "worthy ones." Their Tripitaka establishes fundamental Buddhist teachings on the nature of suffering, the selflessness of persons, the impermanence of all phenomena, and the path of nonviolent ethics and meditation, which leads to liberating wisdom.

The second major Buddhist tradition—which has called itself the Mahayana ("Great Vehicle") because it has seen its teachings as superior to those of the Theravada and the other (now defunct) preceding early Indian schools—developed in the first centuries of the Common Era in North India and Central Asia, and has long since come to be the predominant form of Buddhism followed in the East Asian countries of China, Korea, Vietnam, and Japan. While the content of the Vinaya and Abhidharma portions of its canon is closely modeled (with notable exceptions) on texts from the earlier Indian schools (which Mahayanists have labeled pejoratively as Hinayana, or "Small Vehicle"), the Mahayana also presented a new, divergent scriptural dispensation in its Sutra literature. Composed originally in Sanskrit, these Mahayana Sutras were said to be a higher form of buddha-vacana, which had been kept from the inferior Hinayana Buddhists until the capabilities of humans had evolved enough to employ this more difficult, but also more efficacious, Dharma. Popular texts such as the *Perfection of Wisdom, Lotus, Teaching of Vimalakirti, Flower Garland, Descent into Lanka,* and *Pure Land* Sutras promoted a new spiritual ideal, the career of the paragon figure of compassion and insight, the *bodhisattva* ("enlightenment being"). Focusing on the philosophical and practical tenets espoused in these newly emergent Sutras, the great Indian masters of the first millennium of the Common Era composed explicatory treatises that would come to stand as centerpieces in the Mahayana canons. Most important are the works of the Madhyamika, or "Middle Way," school, which expounded on the central idea of *shunyata,* or "emptiness," and those of the Yogacara ("Yoga Practice") school, which developed influential theories on the mind and its construction of objective realities. The subsequent history of Mahayana as it was transformed in East Asia is a complex and varied one, but in the long run two practically oriented schools, namely the Pure Land and Meditation (commonly known in the West by its Japanese name, Zen) schools, emerged as the most popular and remain so today. These schools supplement their canons with texts containing the discourses and dialogues of their respective patriarchs.

The third Buddhist tradition to appear on the historical scene, beginning around the sixth century C.E., is the Vajrayana ("Thunderbolt Vehicle"), commonly known as Tantric Buddhism. The Vajrayana survives today in the greater Tibetan cultural areas of Asia, including the Himalayan kingdoms of Sikkim, Nepal, and Bhutan. Tantric Buddhists regard themselves as Mahayanists and include in their canon all of the major Mahayana texts mentioned above. However, the Vajrayana itself also claimed a new and divergent dispensation of the

Buddha's word, in the form of texts called Tantras. While not philosophically innovative, the Tantras offered novel systems of meditative disciplines and ritual practices known as *sadhanas*. Followers of the Vajrayana maintain that the Tantras are the highest and final words of the Buddha, esoterically preserved until the circumstances were right for their exposure to humanity. As the name *Vajrayana* suggests, the uniqueness of the Tantras lies in their claim to be providing the most powerful and expeditious means of attaining enlightenment. Like their East Asian Mahayana counterparts, Tantric Buddhists also reserve a place of eminence in their canons for the compositions of their most accomplished masters, who are known as *mahasiddhas*, or "great adepts."

## HINDUISM

What we in the twentieth century call Hinduism is in fact a set of religious practices that have developed over three thousand years of Indian history and have a great variety of textual sources. That history begins with the four Vedas—oral compositions of people who called themselves Aryans and who were the ancestors of many of the inhabitants of India today. The term *Veda* means "knowledge," and these four works make up the accompaniment to Vedic sacrifice—the main form of worship for the early Aryans. Sacrifice usually involved an animal or vegetable offering to one of the many Vedic gods. The first Veda, the *Rig Veda*, is the oldest (c. 1500 B.C.E.), and comprises the mythological hymns of the sacrifice. The second, the *Yajur Veda*, contains directions on how to conduct the ritual; the third, the *Sama Veda*, contains accompanying musical chants. The final Veda, the *Atharva Veda*, includes hymns for fertility, healing, and other everyday uses in the domestic context, apart from the public sacrifice.

The second set of works important to Hinduism is more philosophical in nature. These works are the Upanishads (c.

900–300 B.C.E.), and consist of speculation about the power behind the sacrifice, called *brahman*, and the nature of the sacrificing self, called *atman*. The Upanishads also contain the beginnings of a system of belief in reincarnation—more properly called the transmigration of the individual self—through the endless cycle of births, deaths, and sufferings, called *samsara*. The Upanishadic philosophers believed that the key to liberation from this cycle of suffering was the union between the atman and brahman. Around 200 B.C.E., these initial ideas were developed into an elaborate science of meditation called Yoga by the philosopher Patañjali. His treatise, the *Yoga Sutras*, inaugurated the system of yoga as we know and practice it today.

While the Vedas, Upanishads, and *Yoga Sutras* reflect the religious practices of the upper strata, or castes, of Indian society, there was very little textual evidence for popular religious practices until the emergence of the epics, the *Mahabharata* and the *Ramayana*. The *Mahabharata* is the story of the tragic war between cousins, the Kauravas and the Pandavas. The *Ramayana* depicts the exploits of Rama—a hero said to be the *avatar*, or manifestation, of the god Vishnu. In rescuing his wife Sita from the demon Ravana, Rama slays Ravana and rids the world of the evil. Many see these two epics as the source of popular theology prevalent in India today. They are the first texts that make extensive mention of the classical Hindu pantheon—Shiva, Vishnu, Brahma, and Devi, or the goddess. The *Mahabharata* is also the source of the *Bhagavad Gita*—the *Song to the Lord Krishna*, who, in human form, acts as a charioteer in the war. Particularly in the nineteenth and twentieth centuries, the *Bhagavad Gita* has inspired much popular devotion as a Hindu response to the Christian missionary movement.

Near the end of the period of the composition of the epics (c. 200 C.E.), many kings, especially in North India, began to patronize these popular deities and build temples to house them. Such temples had texts called Puranas attached to them;

the term *purana* literally means "story of the olden times." Puranas are encyclopedic compilations that praised the exploits of particular deities—Vishnu, Shiva, Brahma, and the Devi, mentioned above. Notoriously difficult to date, the Puranas range from 200 C.E. to 1700 C.E. Another important set of texts, called Dharma Shastras, emerged at about this period; these were elaborate law books that codified daily life according to rules concerned with purity and pollution. The most famous of these is the *Manavadharmashastra*, or the *Laws of Manu*. The Puranas and the Dharma Shastras provide the bulk of the material upon which the modern Hindu tradition draws, and they originate in all regions of India.

The wide geographical spread of the Puranas is partly due to the fact that devotional movements were not exclusive to the northern Gangetic plain, where the Vedas and Upanishads were composed, but were inspired equally by the South Indian, or Dravidian, civilizations. These devotional movements were called *bhakti*, literally meaning "belonging to." A *bhakta* is someone who "belongs to" a particular god and has chosen that god for devotion. Beginning in the eighth century C.E., the South Indian bhaktas wrote poetry that became an influential source for Hinduism. The collection of poems by the Tamil saint Nammalvar, the Tiruvaymoli, has attained the same canonical status as the Vedas and is called the Tamil Veda. In addition, the Bengali saint Caitanya inspired a bhakti movement devoted to Krishna in the late fifteenth century C.E.; his followers wrote treatises, among them the *Haribhaktirasamrtasindhu* and *Haribhaktivilasa*, that explain the theology and ritual of devotion to Krishna. Many northern and western Indian poets, such as Mirabai (born c. 1420 C.E.) and Tukaram (1608–1649 C.E.), have contributed significantly to the huge corpus of bhakti poetry and theology that Hindus read and recite today.

The final major source for the study of Hinduism is the

Vedanta philosophical tradition, whose development and systematization is attributed to the teacher Shankara in the ninth century C.E. Shankara, and his major successor, Ramanuja (twelfth century C.E.), developed their philosophy through commentaries, called *bhasyas,* on the two main texts of Vedanta—the *Vedanta Sutras* and the *Brahma Sutras.* These texts summarize the doctrine of the Upanishads, mentioned above. In his classic work, *Brahmasutrabhashya,* Shankara argues a philosophy of nonduality *(advaita).* For him, the perceptions of the mind and the senses are simply *avidya,* ignorance. In ignorance we perceive a duality between subject and object, self and the source of self. This perception of duality prevents the self (atman) from complete identity with brahman. When complete identity is achieved, however, there is liberation of the self from all ignorance.

These manifold sources—the Vedas, the Upanishads, the epics, the Puranas, the Dharma Shastras, the diverse corpus of bhakti poetry, and Vedanta philosophy—make up the spiritual foundations of Hindu practice today.

NOTES

## 1. ISLAM

1. All references from the Qur'an are from A. J. Arberry, *The Koran Interpreted* (New York: Macmillan, 1955).
2. Margaret Smith, "Rabia the Mystic," 45, in Elizabeth Fernea and Basima Bezirgan, eds., *Middle Eastern Muslim Women Speak* (Austin: University of Texas Press, 1977), 45.
3. Huda Lutfi, "Fourteenth-Century Cairene Women," in ibid, 109.
4. Ibid.
5. Abu A'lā Maudūdī, *Purdah and the Status of Women in Islam*, trans. al-Ashari (reprint, Lahore: Islamic Publications, 1992), 176.
6. Ibid., 152.
7. Ibn Ishāq, *Sīrat Rasūl Allāh*, trans. A. Guillaume as *The Life of Muḥammad* (Karachi: Oxford University Press, 1978), 494.
8. Ibid., 495.
9. Ibid., 496.
10. Fatima Mernissi, *The Veil and the Male Elite*, trans. Mary Jo Lakeland (Reading, Mass.: Addison-Wesley, 1991), 7.
11. Ibid., 162.
12. Awad, "The Umm Kulthum Nobody Knows," in Fernea and Bezirgan, *Middle Eastern Women*, 145–46.
13. Valerie Hoffman, "An Islamic Activist: Zeinab al-Ghazali," in *Women and the Family in the Middle East*, ed. Elizabeth Fernea (Austin: University of Texas Press, 1985) 236–37.
14. Elizabeth Fernea, *Guests of the Sheik* (reprint, New York: Doubleday, 1969), 107–9.
15. Rūḥ Allāh Khumaynī, *Islam and Revolution*, trans. Hamid Algar (Berkeley, Calif.: Mizan Press, 1981), 65.

## 2. CHRISTIANITY

1. The translations in this chapter are the author's.
2. Richard A. Horsley, *Archaeology, History, and Society in Galilee: The Social Context of Jesus and the Rabbis* (Valley Forge, Pa.: Trinity Press International, 1996), 89. For his discussion of Nazareth, see pp. 108–30.
3. See Bruce Chilton, "Christianity," in *Evil and Suffering*, Pilgrim Library of World Religions Series, ed. J. Neusner (Cleveland: The Pilgrim Press, 1998).
4. Bruce Chilton, "Opening the Book: Biblical Warrants for the Ordination of Women," *The Modern Churchman* 20, nos.1–2 (1977): 32–35, and "The Gospel of Jesus and the Ministry of Women," *The Modern Churchman* 22.1 (1978–79): 18–21.
5. See Bruce Chilton, *Pure Kingdom: Jesus' Vision of God*, vol. 1, Studying the Historical Jesus (Grand Rapids, Mich.: Eerdmans; London: SPCK, 1996).
6. See Bruce Chilton and Jacob Neusner, *Trading Places: The Intersecting Histories of Judaism and Christianity* (Cleveland: The Pilgrim Press, 1996), 37–58.
7. See Bruce Chilton and Jacob Neusner, *The Intellectual Foundations of Christian and Jewish Discourse: The Philosophy of Religious Argument* (London: Routledge, 1997).
8. Jaroslav Pelikan, *The Christian Tradition: A History of the Development of Doctrine* (Chicago: University of Chicago Press, 1971), 126.
9. See Jean Daniélou and Henri Marrou, *The Christian Centuries*, vol. 1, trans. V. Cronin (New York: McGraw-Hill, 1964), 86–90.
10. See F. L. Cross, *The Early Christian Fathers* (London: Duckworth, 1960), 26.
11. Discussed in Bruce Chilton, "Christianity," in *Sacred Texts and Authority*, ed. Jacob Neusner, Pilgrim Library of World Religions Series (Cleveland: The Pilgrim Press, 1998).
12. See Chilton and Neusner, *Trading Places*, 117–18, and *Trading Places Sourcebook*, 205–36.
13. Cited in *City of God* 16.6.
14. See the translation by Hans-Gebhard Bethge and Orval S. Win-

termute in *The Nag Hammadi Library*, ed. J. M. Robinson (San Francisco: Harper & Row, 1978), 161–79.
15. Elisabeth Schüssler Fiorenza et al., eds., *Searching the Scriptures*, vol. 2, *A Feminist Commentary* (New York: Crossroad, 1994), 4.
16. Ibid.
17. Ibid., 745–46.
18. Ibid., 748.

## 3. JUDAISM

1. The translations in this chapter are the author's.

## 4. HINDUISM

1. This and all other citations from the Manusmrti are taken from *The Laws of Manu*, translated by Wendy Doniger with Brian K. Smith (London: Penguin Books, 1991).
2. Ramayana 2.24.3,4,18; cited and translated in Comelia Dimmitt, "Sita: Fertility Goddess and *Sakti*," in *The Divine Consort: Radha and the Goddesses of India*, ed. John Stratton Hawley and Donna Marie Wulff (Boston: Beacon Press, 1982), 210.
3. Ramayana 5.19.14–16, in ibid., 221.
4. Ramayana 7.48; cited and translated in David Kinsley, *Hindu Goddesses: Visions of the Divine Feminine in the Hindu Religious Tradition* (Berkeley and Los Angeles: University of California Press, 1986), 74.
5. From Jayadeva's *Gitagovinda*, cited and translated by Barbara Stoler Miller, "The Divine Duality of Radha and Krishna," in Hawley and Wulff, *The Divine Consort*, 20.
6. Cited and translated in Edward Dimock and Denise Levertov, trans., *In Praise of Krishna: Songs from the Bengali* (Garden City, N.Y.: Doubleday, 1967), 51.
7. Bhaktamal Nabhadas, cited and translated in John Stratton Hawley and Mark Juergensmeyer, *Songs of the Saints of India* (New York: Oxford University Press, 1988), 123.
8. From the Markandeya Purana, translated by Wendy Doniger O'Flaherty in her *Hindu Myths* (Harmondsworth, Middlesex, Eng.: Penguin Books, 1975), 248–49.

9. From Jadunath Sinha, trans., *Rama Prasada's Devotional Songs: The Cult of Shakti* (Calcutta: Sinha Publishing House, 1966), 3.
10. Ibid., 118–19.
11. Stephanie W. Jamison, *Sacrificed Wife, Sacrificer's Wife: Women, Ritual, and Hospitality in Ancient India* (New York: Oxford University Press, 1996), 254.
12. This and the following passage are from Patrick Olivelle's translation, *Upanishads* (New York: Oxford University Press, 1996), 69–71.
13. The *Stidharmapaddhati* of Tryambakayajvan, 86.4–88.1; translated in I. Julia Lessa, *The Perfect Wife: The Orthodox Hindu Woman according to the Stridharmapaddhati of Tryambakayajvan* (Delhi: Oxford University Press, 1989), 314–15.
14. The *Harsacarita of Bana*, translated by E. B. Cowell and F. W. Thomas (London: Royal Asiatic Society, 1897), 153–55; reprinted in Ainslie T. Embree, ed., *The Hindu Tradition: Readings in Oriental Thought* (New York: Vintage Books, 1966), 98–100.
15. *Vamamarga* III, cited and translated by Agehananda Bharati, *The Tantric Tradition* (New York: Samuel Weiser, 1975), 264.
16. From Barbara Stoler Miller, trans., *The Bhagavad Gita: Krishna's Counsel in Time of War* (New York: Bantam Books, 1986).
17. From the *Mahadeviyakka*, translated by A. K. Ramanujan in his *Speaking of Siva* (Baltimore: Penguin, 1973), 134, 141.
18. Quoted in Anne Mackenzie Pearson, *"Because It Gives Me Peace of Mind": Ritual Fasts in the Religious Lives of Hindu Women* (Albany: State University of New York Press, 1996), 199–200.

## 5. BUDDHISM

1. Margaret Helen Childs, *Rethinking Sorrow: Revelatory Tales of Late Medieval Japan* (Ann Arbor: Center for Japanese Studies, University of Michigan, 1991), 109, 110.
2. Samyutta Nikaya IV.239.
3. Ibid., IV.246.
4. Nichiren Daishonin, *The Major Writings of Nichiren Daishonin*, vol. 5 (Tokyo: Nichiren Shoshu International Center, 1988), 156.

5. Chan Sin-wai, *Buddhism in Late Ch'ing Political Thought* (Hong Kong: Chinese University Press, 1985), 110; quoted in John Strong, *The Experience of Buddhism* (Belmont, Calif.: Wadsworth, 1995), 326.
6. See Carol Gilligan, *In a Different Voice: Psychological Theory and Women's Development* (Cambridge: Harvard University Press, 1982).
7. The original Heinz dilemma is the following:

> In Europe, a woman was near death from cancer. One drug might save her, a form of radium that a druggist in the same town had recently discovered. The druggist was charging two thousand dollars, ten times what the drug cost him to make. The sick woman's husband, Heinz, went to everyone he knew to borrow the money, but he could only get together about half of what it cost. He told the druggist that his wife was dying and asked him to sell it cheaper or let him pay later. But the druggist said, "No." The husband got desperate and broke into the man's store to steal the drug for his wife. Should the husband have done that? Why?
>
> From Lawrence Kohlberg, "Stage and Sequence: The Cognitive-Developmental Approach to Socialization," in *Handbook of Socialization Theory and Research*, ed. D. A. Goslin (Chicago: Rand McNally, 1969), 379.

8. Kalukondayave, quoted in H. L. Seneviratne, *The Work of Kings*, unpublished manuscript, 81–82.
9. Ñanamoli, trans., *The Minor Readings* (Oxford: Pali Text Society, 1991), 148.
10. Samyutta Nikaya, IV.250.
11. *Gradual Sayings (Anguttara Nikaya)*, vol. 3, trans. E. M. Hare (Oxford: Pali Text Society, 1988), III.29–30.
12. This refers to a common assumption in Buddhist communities that moral and spiritual qualities were displayed in bodily appearance.
13. *Jataka*, ed. V. Fausbøll (London: Trubner, 1897), 364–68.
14. Peter Khoroche, trans., *When the Buddha Was a Monkey: Arya*

Sura's *Jatakamala* (Chicago: University of Chicago Press, 1989), 197.
15. Ibid., 203.
16. Ibid., 178.
17. See, for example, Caroline Whitbeck, "A Different Reality: Feminist Ontology," in *Beyond Domination,* ed. Carol Gould (Totowa, N.J.: Rowman and Allanheld, 1984), 64–88.
18. Daiseku Ikeda, "Relationships: My Wife and Comrade," *Mirror Weekly* (Philippines), May 18, 1998, 34.
19. Vidyacakravarti, *Butsarana* (Colombo: Gunasena, 1968), 288.
20. Anguttara Nilcaya IV.92. In the same text, wives are also imaged on models of murderers, thieves, princesses, sisters, friends, and slaves. Those wives who are like mothers, sisters, friends, or slaves are then declared to be best.
21. Ñanamoli, *Minor Readings,* 10.
22. Alex Wayman, trans., *Ethics of Tibet: Bodhisattva Section of Tsong-Kha-Pa's Lam Rim Chen Mo* (Albany: State University of New York Press, 1991), 47.
23. Alan Cole, *Mothers and Sons* (Stanford, Calif.: Stanford University Press, 1998), 181.
24. See the Buddhism chapter in the volume *Evil and Suffering* (Pilgrim Library of World Religions) for a discussion of this passage in another light.
25. Sallie King, "Awakening Stories of Zen Buddhist Women," in *Buddhism in Practice,* ed. Donald S. Lopez Jr. (Princeton, N.J.: Princeton University Press, 1995), 517.
26. King, 520.
27. Susan Murcott, *The First Buddhist Women* (Berkeley, Calif.: Parallax Press, 1991), 117.
28. Paula Arai, "Zen Nuns: Living Treasures of Japanese Buddhism" (Ph.D. diss., Harvard University, 1993), 258.
29. Guanyin is a female future Buddha characterized by her great compassion.
30. The father of Guanyin.
31. This is a reference to the imprisonment of Guanyin by her father

in his palace garden, which he did out of anger at her refusal to marry.
32. Chün-fang Yü, "Chinese Women Pilgrim's Songs Glorifying Guanyin," in *Buddhism in Practice*, ed. Donald S. Lopez Jr. (Princeton, N.J.: Princeton University Press, 1995), 180.
33. Adapted from Paula Arai, "Soto Zen Nuns in Modern Japan," in H. Byron Earhart, *Religion in the Japanese Experience* (Belmont, Calif.: Wadsworth, 1997), 79.
34. John Strong, *The Experience of Buddhism* (Belmont, Calif.: Wadsworth, 1995), 55–56.
35. These are the five precepts all Buddhists undertake to observe.
36. That is, she gives whatever someone requests.
37. *Gradual Sayings*, trans. Hare, IV.178–80; translation slightly modified.
38. See Ibid., II.104–7.
39. Ibid., IV.178–80; translation slightly modified.
40. Upasika Kee Nanayon, *An Unentangled Knowing* (Barre, Mass.: Dhamma Dana Publications, 1995), 60–61.
41. This discussion draws on Barbara Ruch, "The Other Side of Culture in Medieval Japan," in *Cambridge History of Japan*, vol. 3, *Medieval Japan* (Cambridge: Cambridge University Press, 1990), 502–7.

## LITERARY SOURCES OF THE WORLD RELIGIONS

1. A. J. Arberry, *The Koran Interpreted* (New York: Macmillan, 1955).

www.ingramcontent.com/pod-product-compliance
Lightning Source LLC
Chambersburg PA
CBHW050809160426
43192CB00010B/1693